Kids' World Atlas

A Young Person's Guide to the Globe

by Karen Foster and
Felicia Law

Picture Window Books
a capstone imprint

www.capstonepub.com

Published by Capstone Publishers,
151 Good Counsel Drive, P.O. Box 669, Mankato, Minnesota 56002.
www.capstonepub.com

Editors: Jill Kalz and Shelly Lyons
Designers: Hilary Wacholz and Heidi Thompson
Page Production: Ashlee Schultz
Art Director: Nathan Gassman
Content Adviser: Lisa Thornquist, Ph.D., Geography
Cartographer: XNR Productions, Inc.

All books published by Picture Window Books
are manufactured with paper containing at least
10 percent post-consumer waste.

Foster, Karen.
Kids' World Atlas: A Young Person's Guide to the Globe/ by Karen Foster
and Felicia Law. – Mankato, MN: Picture Window Books, 2010
128 p. : col. ill., col. maps : 24 cm
ISBN 978-1-4048-6199-2
G1021
912

Photo Credits:
BigStockPhoto: Kim Seidl, 53; Corbis: Albrecht G. Schaefer, 22t, Alison Wright, 66t, Anders Ryman, cover, Andrew K/epa, 80, Antoine Serra/In Visu, 74-t, Baldev Kapoor/Sygma, 123b, Bernard Annnebicque/Sygma, 88t, Bill Ross, 9, Bill Stormont, 8br, Carl & Ann Purcell, 60t, Charles & Josette Lenars, 19l, Charles O'Rear, 27, Dale C. Spartas, 12, Danny Lehman, 18br, 127tl, David Sutherland, 127bl, 64bl, Derek Cattani, 47, DLILLC, cover, Floris Leeuwenberg/The Cover Story, 51t, Frans Lanting, 24, Free Agents Limited, 65, Fridmar Damm, 23, Gavriel Jecan, 46bl, George H.H. Huey, 8bl, Herve Collart, 61r, Hubert Stadler, 33, Jeffrey L. Rotman, 121br, Jim Zuckerman, 127fr, 26, Kazuyoshi Nomachi, 50b, 54t, 61l, Kelly-Mooney Photography, 10b, Louie Psihoyos, 22b, Louise Gubb, 52r, Martin Harvey, cover, Michael Freeman, 52l, Morton Beebe, 124t, NASA, 10t, Natalie Fobes, 125b, Owen Franken, 46tr, Paul A. Souders, 108t, 40b, Penny Tweedie, 102b, Peter Johnson, 106br, Ralph White, 122b, Remi Benali, 126tl, 54bl, Reuters, 60r, 69, Rob Howard, 51l, Robert Francis/Robert Harding World Imagery, 78b, Ryan Pyle, 64br, Stephen Fink, 121t, Stuart Westmorland, 121bl, Tim Davis, 124b, Tom Nebbia, 60b, Warren Faidley, 82, Yann Arthus-Bertrand, 120, 50t, 66b; Dreamstime: Kurt, compass rose throughout; Image Quest Marine: Peter Batson, 122t; iStockphoto: Sandy Buckley, 125t; Jeff Dozier, 68t; Photographers Direct: James Osmond, 96; Shutterstock: cover, 106t, 81, 89, 92, Chris Howey, 108br, 127br, David MacFarlane, 38br, Denis Babenko, 126tr, 46c, Gary Unwin, 94t, Graeme Knox, 94b, Grigory Kubatyan, 18bl, Ilya Genkin, cover, Jason Maehl, 126br, 78t, jesus parazo, 19r, Jose Alberto Tejo, 32b, Kharidehal Abhirama Ashwin, cover, Louie Schoeman, 38bl, Marco Regalia, 8tr, Medvedev Vladimir, 79, Natalia Sinjushina & Evgeniy Meyke, 67, Nicholas Rjabow, 102t, 126cl, Nik Niklz, 108bl, Oleg Kozlov, 37r, Ricky Subiantoputra, 123t, Sander van Sinttruye, 93, Shannon West, 18tr, Tan Kian Khoon, cover, Vishal Shah, 68b, 74-b, Walter S. Becker, 13, Wendy Shiao, 88b; Still Pictures: Xavier Eichaker/Biosphoto, 64t; Superstock: Age Fotostock, 106bl; TopFoto: 25l, cover, Fiore, 32t, HIP, 37l, ImageWorks, 25r, 38tr, 40t, Topham/Woodmansterne, 36.

Editor's Note: The maps in this book were created with the Miller projection.

Table of Contents

Welcome to the World

The world is made up of seven continents: North America, South America, Europe, Africa, Asia, Australia, and Antarctica.

Arctic Circle

NORTH AMERICA

Atlantic Ocean

Tropic of Cancer

Pacific Ocean

Equator

SOUTH AMERICA

Tropic of Capricorn

Legend
A legend tells you the title of a map and what the map's symbols mean.

SOUTH AMERICA	Continent
Pacific Ocean	Ocean

Antarctic Circle

The Antarctic Circle is an imaginary line in the southern part of the world that marks the edge of the Antarctic region.

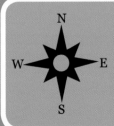

Compass Rose
A compass rose shows you the four cardinal directions: north (N), south (S), east (E), and west (W).

The world has five oceans:
Atlantic, Pacific, Indian, Arctic,
and Southern.

North Pole

Arctic Ocean

The Arctic Circle is an imaginary line in the northern part of the world that marks the edge of the Arctic region.

Arctic Circle

EUROPE

ASIA

The Tropic of Cancer and the Tropic of Capricorn are imaginary lines north and south of the equator. Places that lie between the two lines are hot and wet.

Tropic of Cancer

Pacific Ocean

AFRICA

Indian
Ocean

Equator

The equator is an imaginary line around the middle of the world.

AUSTRALIA

Tropic of Capricorn

Southern Ocean

Antarctic Circle

ANTARCTICA

Scale Bar

A scale bar helps measure distance. It tells you the difference between distances on a map and the actual distances on Earth's surface.

Miles
0   0.5   1   1.5   2   2.5

0   1   2   3   4
Kilometers

South Pole

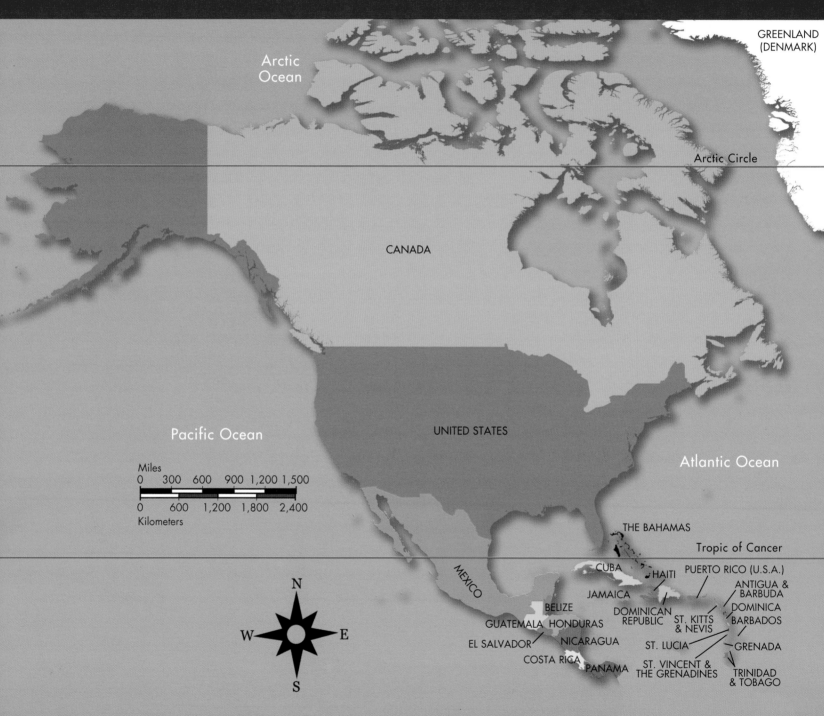

GREENLAND
(DENMARK)

Arctic
Ocean

Arctic Circle

CANADA

Pacific Ocean

Miles
0   300   600   900 1,200 1,500

0   600   1,200 1,800 2,400
Kilometers

UNITED STATES

Atlantic Ocean

THE BAHAMAS

Tropic of Cancer

CUBA
HAITI   PUERTO RICO (U.S.A.)

MEXICO
JAMAICA   ANTIGUA &
                                  BARBUDA
BELIZE   DOMINICAN   DOMINICA
              REPUBLIC ST. KITTS BARBADOS
GUATEMALA HONDURAS   & NEVIS
EL SALVADOR   NICARAGUA   ST. LUCIA   GRENADA

COSTA RICA   ST. VINCENT &
           PANAMA   THE GRENADINES   TRINIDAD
                                          & TOBAGO

N
W   E
S

ANTIGUA AND BARBUDA

THE BAHAMAS

BARBADOS

BELIZE

CANADA

COSTA RICA

CUBA

DOMINICA

DOMINICAN REPUBLIC

EL SALVADOR

GRENADA

GUATEMALA

HAITI

HONDURAS

JAMAICA

MEXICO

NICARAGUA

PANAMA

SAINT KITTS AND NEVIS

SAINT LUCIA

SAINT VINCENT AND THE GRENADINES

TRINIDAD AND TOBAGO

UNITED STATES

Continent size: the third-largest of Earth's seven continents

Number of countries: 23

Major languages: English, French, Spanish

Total population: 534 million (2009 estimate)

Largest country (land size): Canada

Most populated country: United States

Most populated city: Mexico City, Mexico

Climate: mostly mild and continental; polar in Greenland and northern Canada; dry in the West; tropical in the South; cool to cold in the mountains

Highest point: Mount McKinley, United States, 20,320 feet (6,198 meters)

Lowest point: Death Valley, United States, 282 feet (86 m) below sea level

Longest river: Mississippi River

Largest body of water: Lake Superior

Largest desert: Great Basin Desert

Major agricultural products: beans, coffee, corn, cotton, dairy products, soybeans, sugar/sugarcane, tropical fruits, wheat

Major industries: agriculture, fishing, forestry, mining, manufacturing (machinery, clothing, paper, electronics, chemicals, and motor vehicles)

Natural resources: coal, copper, gold, iron ore, natural gas, nickel, oil, silver

North America's Landforms

The land of North America takes many shapes—from mountains to deep canyons to low-lying plains.

The peaks of the Rocky Mountains, or Rockies, stretch through the western region of North America about 2,000 miles (3,200 kilometers) into Mexico. In Mexico, the mountains are called the Sierra Madre Oriental and the Sierra Madre Occidental.

Parts of North America stick out into the ocean as peninsulas, while other parts are completely surrounded by water.

A smoking mountain

A volcano is a kind of mountain that can throw hot, melted rock (lava), ashes, and gases from inside Earth. Mexico has many volcanoes. Popocatépetl is one of the active ones. Although it smokes, the mountaintop is covered with snow all year long.

The name Popocatépetl means "smoking mountain."

Mesas

Flat-topped towers of layered rock called mesas are found in the deserts and canyons of the southwestern United States.

The word mesa means "table" in Spanish.

Grand Canyon

North America's Grand Canyon is the largest canyon in the world. Its deep valley was carved out by the Colorado River. The steep sides of the canyon are made from layers of rock. Some of the rocks are about 2 billion years old.

At sunset, the rock walls of the Grand Canyon seem to change color.

- Mount McKinley is not only the highest mountain in the United States, it's also the highest mountain in North America.
- Greenland is the largest island in the world.
- Canada has the world's longest coastline.

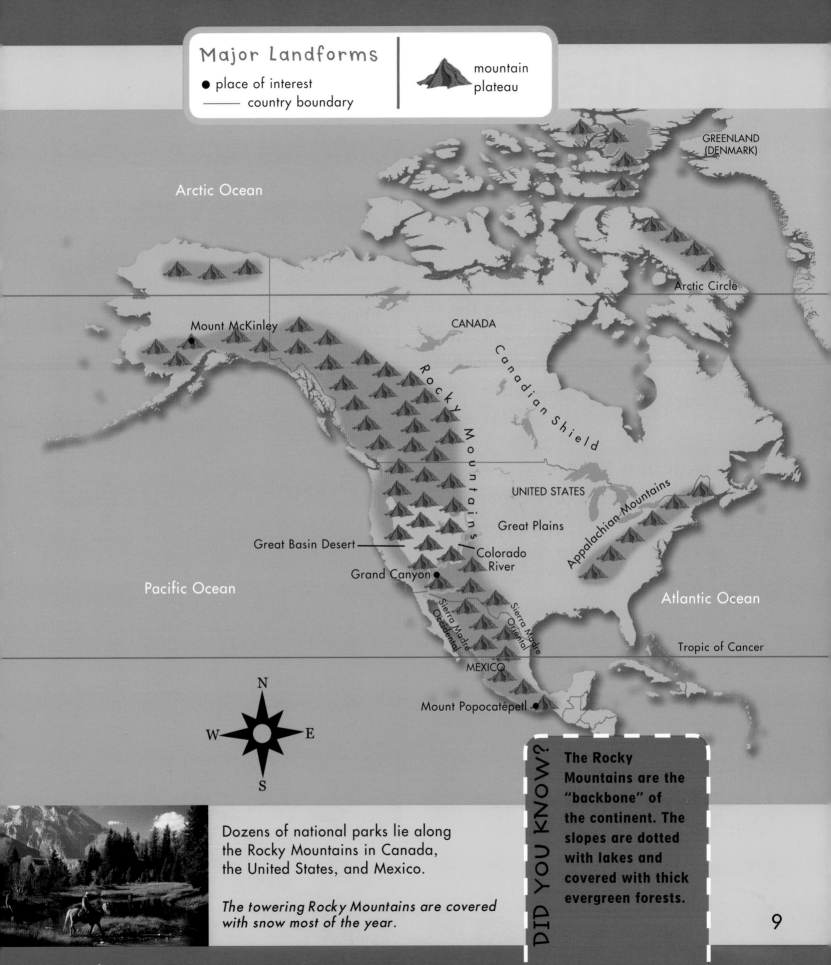

Major Landforms

- ● place of interest
- —— country boundary

mountain
plateau

Arctic Ocean

GREENLAND
(DENMARK)

Arctic Circle

Mount McKinley ●

CANADA

Rocky Mountains

Canadian Shield

UNITED STATES

Great Plains

Appalachian Mountains

Great Basin Desert ——

Colorado
River

Grand Canyon ●

Sierra Madre
Occidental

Sierra Madre
Oriental

Pacific Ocean

Atlantic Ocean

Tropic of Cancer

MEXICO

Mount Popocatépetl ●

N
W   E
S

Dozens of national parks lie along
the Rocky Mountains in Canada,
the United States, and Mexico.

*The towering Rocky Mountains are covered
with snow most of the year.*

DID YOU KNOW?

The Rocky
Mountains are the
"backbone" of
the continent. The
slopes are dotted
with lakes and
covered with thick
evergreen forests.

North America has many large rivers and lakes. Canada has more lakes and inland water than any other country in the world.

The Mississippi River and the Missouri River flow across the lower half of the continent. These two major rivers are the longest rivers in North America.

The Niagara River

The Niagara River flows from Lake Erie to Lake Ontario, a distance of just 35 miles (56 kilometers). It serves as part of the border between the United States and Canada. At the river's midway point, water spills over a steep cliff, forming Niagara Falls.

A tour boat sails past the spray of Niagara Falls.

The Great Lakes

The Great Lakes are the largest group of freshwater lakes on Earth. They form part of the border between Canada and the United States. The five Great Lakes, from west to east, are Superior, Michigan, Huron, Erie, and Ontario. Lake Superior is the largest freshwater lake in the world.

Lake Michigan (bottom left) looks like a long, blue finger when viewed from space.

Lake Nicaragua

Lake Nicaragua is the largest freshwater lake in Central America. It is about 100 miles (160 km) long and up to 45 miles (72 km) wide. Once part of the Caribbean Sea, the lake is home to many saltwater fish that have adapted to their new surroundings.

10

- Salt Lake City, United States, is built on the dried-out bed of a huge salt lake.
- The Rio Grande forms a natural border between part of Mexico and the United States. The river supplies water to the surrounding land, making it easier for people to grow crops in the dry soil.

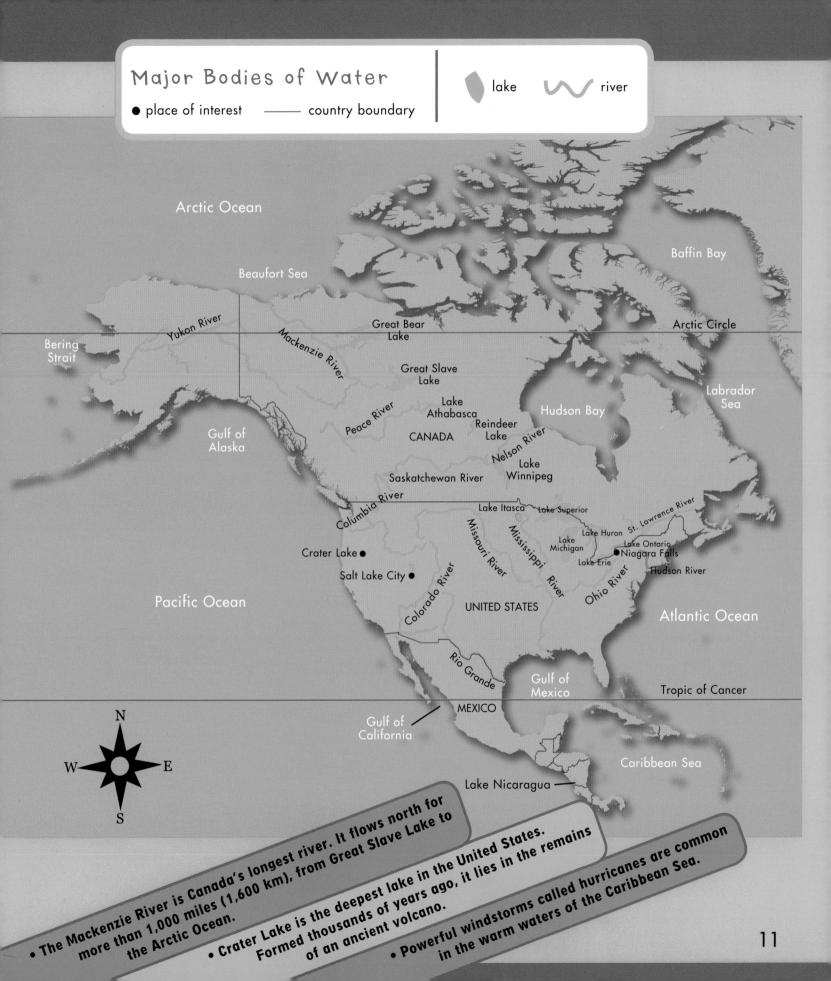

Major Bodies of Water

- place of interest
— country boundary

lake   river

Arctic Ocean

Baffin Bay

Beaufort Sea

Arctic Circle

Yukon River

Great Bear Lake

Mackenzie River

Bering Strait

Great Slave Lake

Labrador Sea

Gulf of Alaska

Lake Athabasca

Reindeer Lake

Hudson Bay

Peace River

CANADA

Nelson River

Lake Winnipeg

Saskatchewan River

Columbia River

Lake Itasca

Lake Superior

St. Lawrence River

Lake Huron

Missouri River

Mississippi River

Lake Michigan

Lake Ontario

Niagara Falls

Crater Lake •

Lake Erie

Hudson River

Salt Lake City •

Colorado River

Ohio River

Pacific Ocean

UNITED STATES

Atlantic Ocean

Rio Grande

Gulf of Mexico

Tropic of Cancer

N
W E
S

MEXICO

Gulf of California

Caribbean Sea

Lake Nicaragua

- The Mackenzie River is Canada's longest river. It flows north for more than 1,000 miles (1,600 km), from Great Slave Lake to the Arctic Ocean.

- Crater Lake is the deepest lake in the United States. Formed thousands of years ago, it lies in the remains of an ancient volcano.

- Powerful windstorms called hurricanes are common in the warm waters of the Caribbean Sea.

North America's Climate

Climate is the average weather a place has from season to season, year to year. Rainfall and temperature play large parts in a region's climate.

Because North America stretches from above the Arctic Circle to below the Tropic of Cancer, it has a wide range of climates.

The United States is so large that it has six different kinds of climate. Its northern-most places have a cold polar climate, while its southern-most places have a hot tropical climate.

Hot and cold

The continent of North America has some of the hottest and coldest temperatures on Earth. In July 1913, Death Valley, United States, recorded the second-hottest temperature in the world. It was 134 degrees Fahrenheit (57 degrees Celsius). In February 1947, Snag, in far northwestern Canada, recorded the third-coldest temperature on Earth. It was minus 81 F (minus 63 C).

Continental climate

Much of Canada and one-fourth of the United States has a continental climate. This region has four separate seasons: a cool spring and fall, a warm to hot summer, and a cold winter. In fall, when the weather gets colder, the leaves of trees such as maple and birch turn red and gold and drop to the ground.

Maple trees are the most colorful in fall.

Climate basics

A region's climate depends upon three major things: how close it is to the ocean, how high up it is, and how close it is to the equator. Areas along the ocean have milder climates than areas farther inland. The higher a region is, and the farther it is from the equator, the colder its temperature.

- Panama is North America's southern-most country. Because it lies close to the equator, temperatures average a warm 80 F (27 C) year-round.

- Most of Central America has a tropical climate. Some areas receive more than 240 inches (610 centimeters) of rain each year.

- The islands in the Caribbean Sea have hot, wet summers and warm, fairly dry winters. The islands' wettest months are May through October.

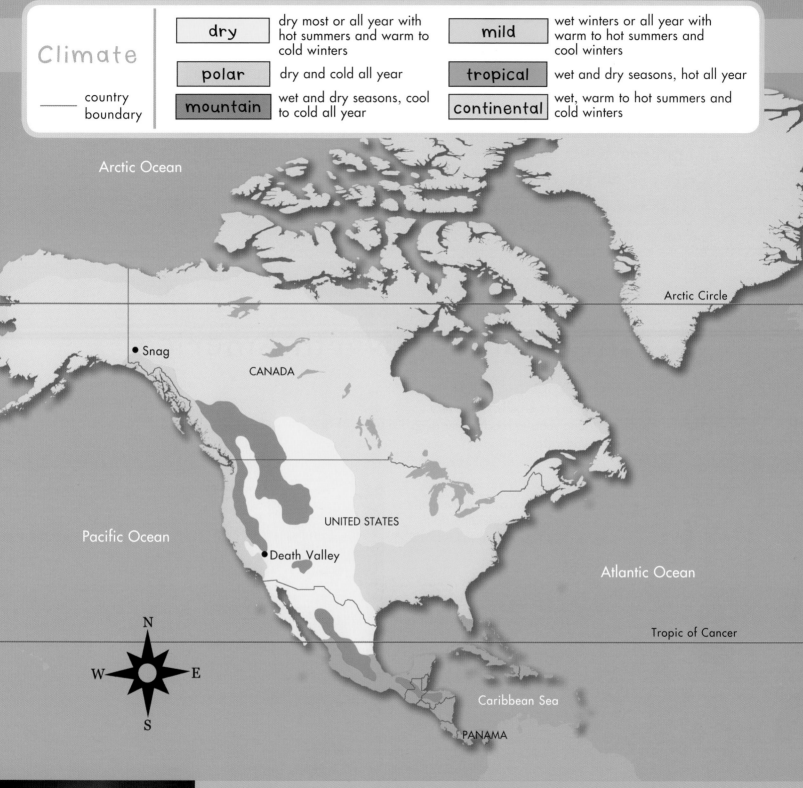

Climate

country boundary

dry	dry most or all year with hot summers and warm to cold winters	
polar	dry and cold all year	
mountain	wet and dry seasons, cool to cold all year	
mild	wet winters or all year with warm to hot summers and cool winters	
tropical	wet and dry seasons, hot all year	
continental	wet, warm to hot summers and cold winters	

Arctic Ocean

Arctic Circle

• Snag

CANADA

Pacific Ocean

UNITED STATES

• Death Valley

Atlantic Ocean

N
W E
S

Tropic of Cancer

Caribbean Sea

PANAMA

In the far northern parts of North America, the Arctic winter is long, dark, and cold. At night, the sky often lights up with shimmering colors known as the northern lights.

The northern lights glow in many different colors.

13

North America's Plants

Because of its many ecosystems, North America is home to a wide variety of plants. An ecosystem is all of the living and nonliving things in a certain area. It includes plants, animals, soil, weather ... everything!

Plants such as cactuses have adapted to the hot, dry conditions of North America's desert ecosystems by storing water. Prairie grasses have deep roots so they can survive wildfires. Forests of evergreens, maples, and other hardy trees can be found across one-third of the continent.

Some Plants of North America

desert

	mesquite bush	The spiky mesquite bush grows in dry riverbeds. It has very long roots to reach water deep underground.
	saguaro cactus	The saguaro cactus is the world's largest cactus, standing up to 50 feet (15 meters) tall.

forest

	pine tree	Pine trees are a type of evergreen tree called a conifer. They have needle-like leaves and produce cones.
	cranberry	Cranberry creeps over the floor of the northern forests. It has pink flowers and red berries.
	redwood tree	The redwoods are some of the oldest trees in North America. They are also the world's tallest. Their reddish trunks can tower up to 330 feet (101 m) into the sky.

grassland

	grasses	Central North America is covered with grasses such as buffalo grass and Kentucky bluegrass. The summer sun is so hot that dry grasslands can catch fire.

rain forest

	trumpet creeper	The colorful trumpet creeper climbs on trees in the rain forests of Central America.
	rubber tree	Rubber trees also grow in the rain forest. A sticky juice from the tree is used to make rubber.

tundra

	moss	Across the tundra, small plants such as moss and lichen cling to the hard, bare ground.
	dwarf willow	The dwarf willow is the smallest tree in the world. It grows only 4 inches (10 centimeters) tall.

14

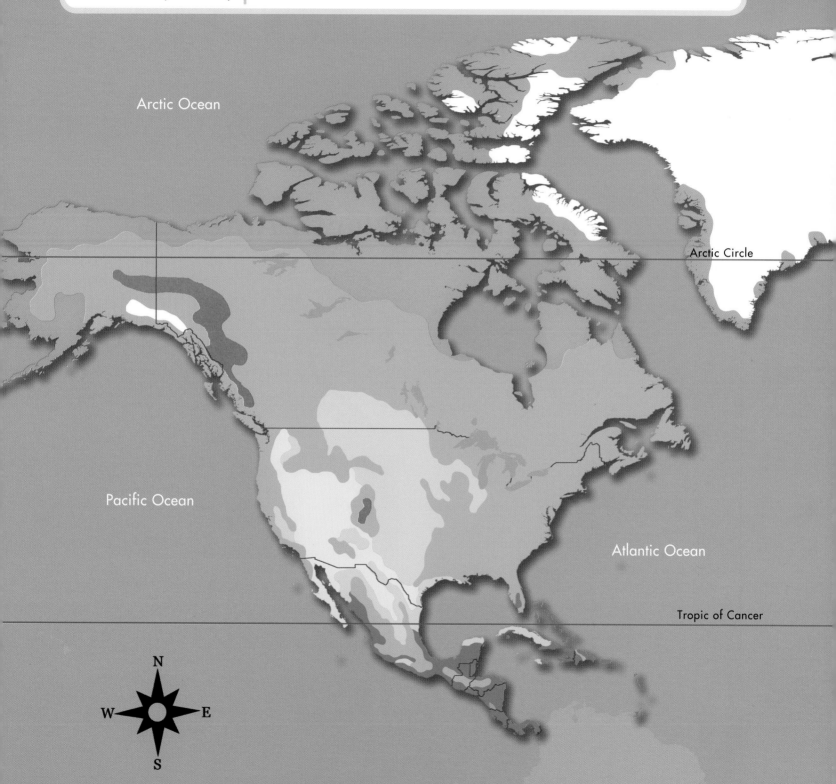

Major Ecosystems

—— country boundary

| desert | grassland | mountain | tundra |
| forest | ice cap | rain forest | wetlands |

Arctic Ocean

Arctic Circle

Pacific Ocean

Atlantic Ocean

Tropic of Cancer

N
W   E
S

North America's Animals

Many different types of animals live in North America, and they are all well-adapted to the ecosystems in which they live. An ecosystem is all of the living and nonliving things in a certain area.

Moose, bears, and other animals that live in North America's tundra ecosystems have thick fur to keep them warm through the long winters. In the desert, animals such as coyotes have light-colored fur that reflects the hot sunlight and keeps them cool.

Some Animals of North America

desert	coyote	Coyotes hunt for small animals, such as jackrabbits and mice.	
forest	goose	In the spring, geese fly north to nesting grounds in Canada. In the fall, they fly south to spend the winter in sunny Mexico.	
	beaver	The beaver cuts down trees with its strong teeth and builds dams in streams and rivers.	
	puma	Pumas are large wild cats that can live in a variety of ecosystems, including forests, mountains, and grasslands.	
	bald eagle	The bald eagle can be found across Canada and the United States. It lives near water where there are fish to eat. It also needs tall trees to nest in.	

grassland	prairie dog	Prairie dogs are small, furry squirrel-like animals that live in burrows underground.	
	monarch butterfly	Each year, hundreds of monarch butterflies fly from summer homes in Canada to winter in Mexico.	
rain forest	toucan	The toucan is a fruit-eating bird with a huge, yellow bill. It lives high in the rain forest trees.	
tundra	grizzly bear	Grizzlies are very large brown bears. They eat fruit, honey, berries, and small animals.	
	moose	The moose is a large deer with humped shoulders and huge antlers. It lives in the snowy forests and swamps of the North.	
wetlands	American alligator	American alligators are found in rivers, swamps, ponds, and other watery areas of the southeastern United States.	

16

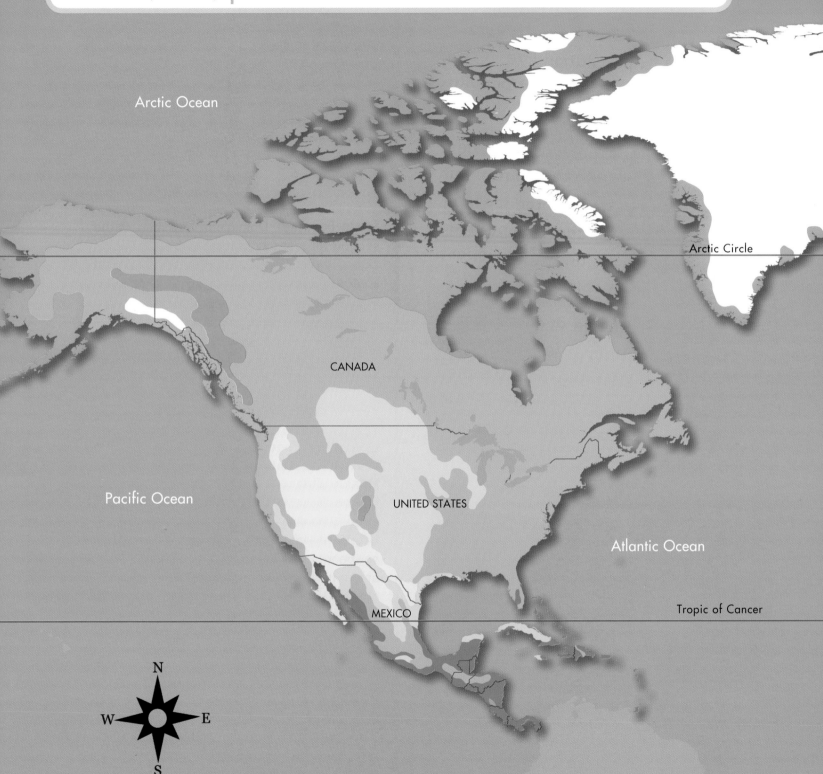

Major Ecosystems

country boundary

desert · grassland · mountain · tundra
forest · ice cap · rain forest · wetlands

Arctic Ocean

Arctic Circle

CANADA

Pacific Ocean

UNITED STATES

Atlantic Ocean

MEXICO

Tropic of Cancer

N
W E
S

North America's Population

More than two-thirds of North America's population live in cities. Mexico City is the most populated city on the continent.

Most North Americans live near bodies of water. The water can be used for power, for jobs, and for fun. It can also be used to grow crops and to transport goods and people.

There are large areas in North America where very few people live. For example, few people want to live in northern Canada, where the winters are long, cold, and dark.

Half of Guatemala's population lives in Guatemala City, the country's capital and the largest city in Central America.

Four important cities

San Francisco, United States, is home to about 808,000 people. One of the city's most famous areas is Chinatown. Many Chinese families live there.

A typical building in Chinatown, San Francisco

Santo Domingo, Dominican Republic, is the second-largest city in the Caribbean (Havana, Cuba, is the largest). Located on the country's southern coast, the city of about 3 million people is a major port.

Montréal is a busy Canadian port city. Located on the banks of the St. Lawrence River, Montréal is a center for industry, business, and culture. Nearly 3.5 million people live there.

One of the biggest cities in the world, **Mexico City**, Mexico, is home to about 20 million people. It was built on the site of an ancient Aztec city called Tenochtitlan.

The lights of Mexico City

- Aside from the West Coast, few people live in the western half of the United States. The land is used mostly for farming, ranching, and recreation.

- In most Central American and Caribbean countries, about half of the population lives in the countries' capital cities.

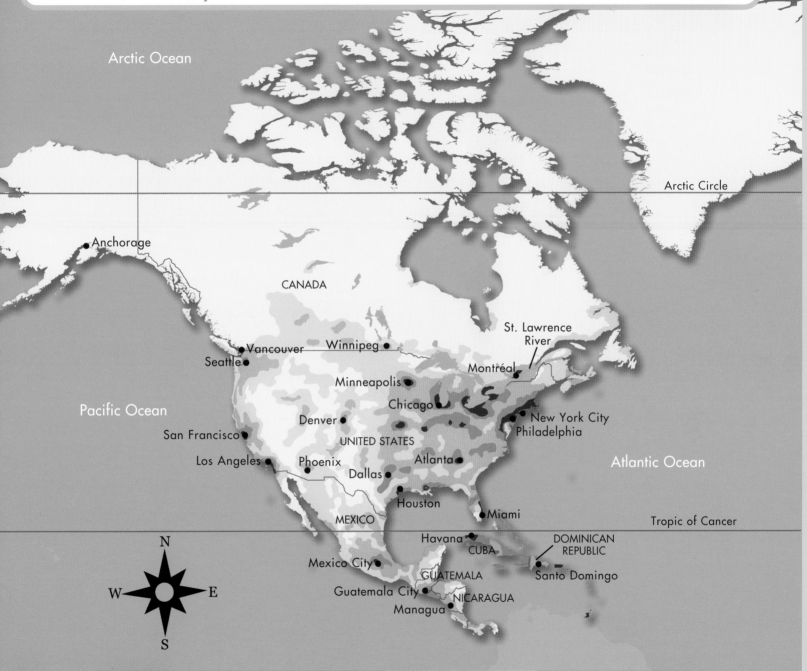

People per Square Mile

- ● place of interest
- — country boundary

| less than 5 | 5-25 | 25-125 | 125-250 | more than 250 |

Arctic Ocean

Arctic Circle

Anchorage

CANADA

Pacific Ocean

Vancouver
Seattle
Winnipeg
St. Lawrence River
Montréal
Minneapolis
Chicago
Denver
New York City
Philadelphia
San Francisco
UNITED STATES
Atlantic Ocean
Los Angeles
Phoenix
Atlanta
Dallas
Houston
MEXICO
Miami
Tropic of Cancer
Havana
CUBA
DOMINICAN REPUBLIC
Mexico City
Santo Domingo
GUATEMALA
Guatemala City
NICARAGUA
Managua

N
W E
S

Besides the Inuit, very few people live in northern North America.

The Inuit live in villages near and inside the cold Arctic Circle.

More than half of the U.S. population lives in large cities along the coasts.

Southern U.S. coastlines are often lined with buildings.

19

CHAPTER TWO

South America

VENEZUELA

GUYANA
SURINAME
FRENCH
GUIANA

COLOMBIA

Equator

ECUADOR

PERU

BRAZIL

BOLIVIA

PARAGUAY

Pacific Ocean

CHILE

URUGUAY

Atlantic Ocean

ARGENTINA

N
W E
S

Miles
0   200   400   600   800   1,000
0   400   800   1,200   1,600
Kilometers

ARGENTINA BOLIVIA BRAZIL

CHILE COLOMBIA ECUADOR

FRENCH GUIANA GUYANA PARAGUAY

PERU SURINAME URUGUAY

VENEZUELA

Continent size: the fourth-largest of Earth's seven continents

Number of countries: 13

Major languages: Spanish, Portuguese, English, French, Native American languages

Total population: 386 million (2009 estimate)

Largest country (land size): Brazil

Most populated country: Brazil

Most populated city: São Paulo, Brazil

Climate: humid, tropical climate along the equator; mild in the Southeast and along the southwestern coast; dry in the South with hot summers and warm to cold winters; cool to cold in the mountains

Highest point: Mount Aconcagua, Argentina, 22,834 feet (6,964 meters)

Lowest point: Valdés Peninsula, Argentina, 132 feet (40 m) below sea level

Longest river: Amazon River

Largest body of water: Lake Maracaibo

Largest desert: Patagonian Desert

Major agricultural products: bananas, beef, cocoa beans, coffee, corn, cotton, cut flowers, dairy products, grapes, rice, soybeans, sugarcane, wheat

Major industries: fishing, lumber, oil, manufacturing (consumer goods such as clothing, beverages, motor vehicles, electrical and mechanical equipment, and plastics)

Natural resources: bauxite, copper, gemstones, iron, lead, manganese, natural gas, oil, tin, zinc

South America's Landforms

The land of South America takes many shapes—from mountains to deep canyons and from high, flat plateaus to low-lying plains, islands, and peninsulas.

The peaks of the Andes Mountains stretch down the western side of South America. The highlands in the east are also high and rugged. To the south lie grassy lowlands and higher plains called plateaus. They stretch down to Tierra del Fuego, a group of islands at the continent's tip.

Snow-covered Andes

There are many snow-covered peaks in the Andes. Some are the cones of volcanoes. A volcano is a kind of mountain that can spew out lava, ashes, and hot gases from deep inside the earth. Most of these volcanoes no longer erupt, but some still do.

Gorges

Narrow, steep-sided valleys, called gorges, cut through the Guiana Highlands. The gorges were made by fast-flowing rivers wearing away the highland rock.

A gorge in the Guiana Highlands

Avenue of volcanoes

More than 30 volcanoes form a line, or "avenue," down the middle of Ecuador. One of these, Mount Cotopaxi, is the world's tallest active volcano.

An active volcano darkens the sky over Ecuador.

The highest peak

The highest peak in the Andes is called Aconcagua. Not only is it the highest peak in South America, it is also the highest peak located outside of Asia. Rising 22,834 feet (6,964 meters), Mount Aconcagua lies near the Argentinean/Chilean border.

• The Brazilian Highlands stretch down part of the country's eastern coast.

• The Andes Mountains are the second-highest mountains in the world. The Himalayas, in Asia, are the highest.

22

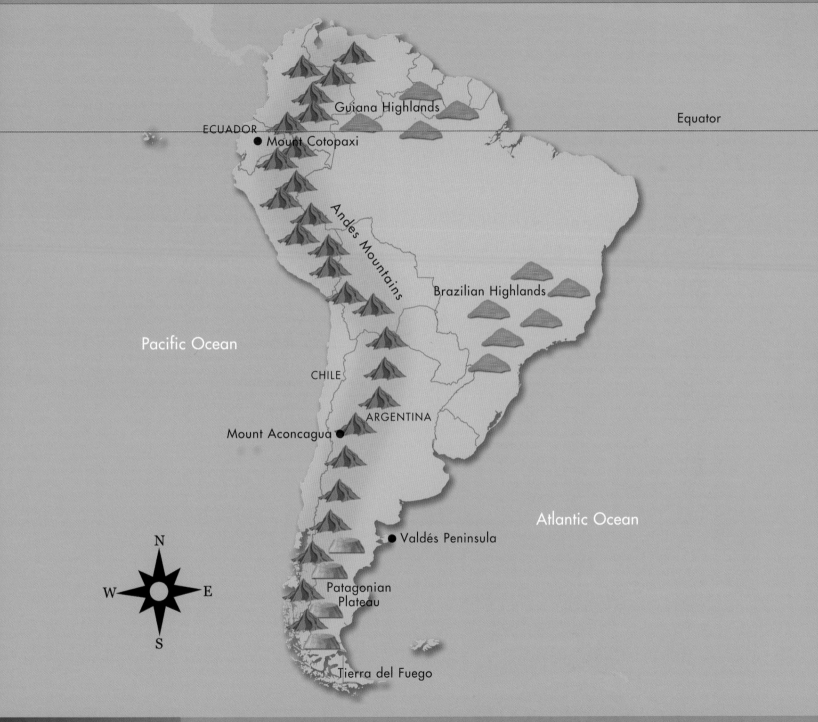

Equator

ECUADOR
● Mount Cotopaxi

Guiana Highlands

Andes Mountains

Brazilian Highlands

Pacific Ocean

CHILE

ARGENTINA

Mount Aconcagua ●

Atlantic Ocean

● Valdés Peninsula

N
W   E
S

Patagonian
Plateau

Tierra del Fuego

The Patagonian Plateau is a flat, dry, bare stretch of land in southern Argentina. Some of the oldest rocks on Earth can be found there.

The Patagonian Plateau lies in the shadow of the Andes Mountains.

23

South America's Bodies of Water

The Amazon River is the world's second-longest river. Apart from the main river, or branch, running from west to east, the Amazon has 1,000 tributaries. Tributaries are smaller rivers that feed larger ones.

The continent is also crisscrossed by many other large rivers. The Parana and Madeira rivers are the largest of these.

The Amazon River

The Amazon River starts as a small stream high in the Andes. It flows 4,000 miles (6,400 kilometers) across South America to the Atlantic Ocean. The Amazon carries more freshwater than any other river in the world.

Some parts of the Amazon River are yellow because they carry a lot of silt (sand and dirt).

A "golden" lake

Lake Guatavita, in the mountains of Colombia, is believed to hold treasure. Legends tell how gold and gemstones were thrown into the water long ago by the Chibcha people. The treasures were gifts to their lake god, El Dorado, or "golden man." But the treasure has never been found.

Mighty women

In 1541, Spanish sailors exploring a river in South America were attacked by a group of native women. The women were very strong and fought hard. The Spaniards later named the river "Amazon," after a group of strong women fighters in a famous Greek legend.

A giant waterway

There is a plan to deepen three of South America's main rivers. This project would form a waterway running almost the full length of the continent. Large ships could then reach inland places far from the coast.

• The huge Itaipu Dam, on the Parana River, is the largest dam in the world.

• Lake Maracaibo, in northwestern Venezuela, is South America's largest natural lake.

Major Bodies of Water

• place of interest — country boundary

🔷 lake 〰 river

Lake Maracaibo ◆ VENEZUELA
Orinoco River

Lake Guatavita ●
COLOMBIA

● Angel Falls

Equator

Amazon River

Madeira River

PERU

Lake Titicaca

BOLIVIA

Parana River

Pacific Ocean

● Itaipu
Dam

ARGENTINA

Atlantic Ocean

N
W   E
S

Lake Titicaca is the world's highest lake that ships can sail on. It lies on the border between Bolivia and Peru.

Handwoven reed boats sail across the calm waters of Lake Titicaca.

In Venezuela, a tributary of the Orinoco River drops 3,212 feet (980 meters), forming the world's highest waterfall—Angel Falls.

Angel Falls

25

South America's Climate

Much of South America has a tropical climate. Temperatures are hot all year. Rain is seasonal.

But some parts of the continent have dry, mild, or mountain climates. More than half of South America's countries have more than one climate.

Climate is the average weather a place has from season to season, year to year. Rainfall and temperature play large parts in a region's climate.

Seasonal rains

A tropical climate has two seasons: rainy and dry. During the dry season, land surrounding rivers may be covered with swampy forests. But during the wet season, when the rivers flood, the forests may disappear underwater.

Dry land

Parts of northern Chile haven't seen rain for 400 years! The few plants and animals that live there must get their water from mountain snow, fog, and dew.

Cloud forests

Cloud forests are common in the mountain climate of South America. These clouds form when hot air from the Pacific Ocean rises over the mountains and cools. The clouds are so low that the treetops rise above them.

Cloud forests are often seen along the western part of South America.

Climate basics

A region's climate depends upon three major things: how close it is to the ocean, how high up it is, and how close it is to the equator. Areas along the ocean have milder climates than areas farther inland. The higher a region is, and the farther it is from the equator, the colder its temperature.

- The largest desert in South America is the Patagonian. It is a cold desert. Most of the desert's precipitation (water) falls in the form of snow.
- Areas in South America with a tropical climate may receive more than 80 inches (2 meters) of rain each year.
- The Atacama Desert, in northern Chile, is the driest place on Earth.

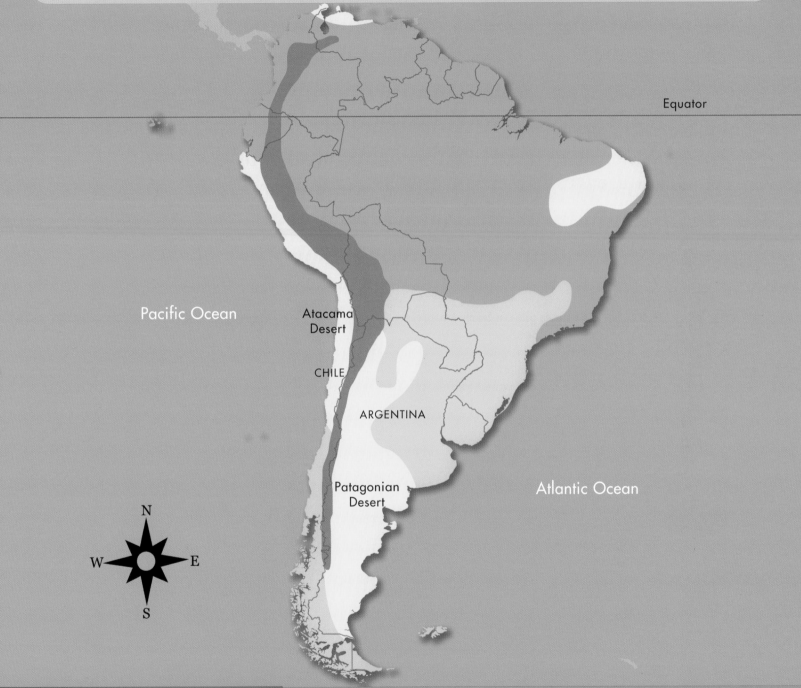

Climate

country boundary

dry	dry most or all year with hot summers and warm to cold winters
tropical	wet and dry seasons, hot all year
mild	wet winters or all year with warm to hot summers and cool winters
mountain	wet and dry seasons, cool to cold all year

Equator

Pacific Ocean

Atacama Desert

CHILE

ARGENTINA

Patagonian Desert

Atlantic Ocean

N
W E
S

Country of many climates

Chile has many different climates. The southern half of the country has a mild climate. The northern half has a dry climate. Regions along Chile's eastern border have a mountain climate.

Grapes grow well in Chile's mild climate.

27

South America's Plants

Of South America's many ecosystems, the rain forest is the one most people think of first. An ecosystem is all of the living and nonliving things in a certain area. It includes plants, animals, soil, weather ... everything!

The Amazon Rain Forest is the largest rain forest in the world. It is more than one-third the size of the mainland United States! This amazing ecosystem is like a giant greenhouse, filled with countless trees, flowers, vines, and other plants.

Some Plants of South America

desert

cactus

Cactuses grow in South America's deserts. Because little rain falls, the plants must spread their roots just below the ground to take in what water they can.

mountain

moss

Moss covers the mountain rocks. Only tiny, low-lying plants can survive the harsh, snowy winters of the mountains.

grassland

grasses

The Pampas are large stretches of open grassland that cover parts of southeastern South America. Only tough, spiky grasses can grow there. Grasses also grow in the Pantanal, which is one of the world's largest freshwater wetlands.

rain forest

Brazil nut tree

Brazil nut trees are among the tallest trees in the Amazon Rain Forest. A single tree can be home to hundreds of animals, birds, and insects.

rubber tree

Rubber trees also grow in the rain forest. A sticky juice from the tree is used to make rubber.

vanilla orchid

Vanilla orchids grow in the topmost part of the rain forest. Their seeds are crushed to make vanilla flavoring.

Major Ecosystems

—— country boundary

| desert | grassland | rain forest | wetlands |
| forest | mountain | tundra |

Equator

A m a z o n
R a i n F o r e s t

Pantanal

Pacific Ocean

Pampas

Atlantic Ocean

Patagonia

N
W   E
S

South America's Animals

More than half of Earth's plant and animal species live in South America, especially in the Amazon Rain Forest. All are well-adapted to the ecosystems in which they live. An ecosystem is all of the living and nonliving things in a certain area.

Animals of South America include mammals such as monkeys, jaguars, and sloths; birds such as toucans, parrots, and owls; reptiles such as snakes, turtles, and lizards; many kinds of fish; and thousands and thousands of insect species.

Some Animals of South America

grassland	giant anteater	The giant anteater uses its narrow snout to suck ants and termites from their nests. Wild giant anteaters live in the grasslands and forests of Central and South America.
mountain	condor	The condor flies hundreds of miles each day, hunting for food.
mountain	llama	Llamas live in herds on the high mountain slopes.
rain forest	parrot	Parrots use bright feathers to find a mate in the dark forest.

rain forest	jaguar	The jaguar hunts small monkeys and birds in the jungle.
rain forest	piranha	Piranhas attack their prey with razor-sharp teeth. These fish are found in the Amazon and other freshwater rivers.
rain forest	blue morpho	The blue morpho butterfly is the size of a child's hand. This butterfly is found only in Central and South America.
rain forest	sloth	The sleepy sloth hangs upside down in the trees and hardly moves at all.
rain forest	toucan	The toucan is a fruit-eating bird with a huge, yellow bill.
rain forest	poison tree frog	The poison tree frog's bright red coloring warns enemies to stay away.

Major Ecosystems

— country boundary

desert grassland rain forest wetlands

forest mountain tundra

Equator

Amazon
Rain Forest

Pacific Ocean

Atlantic Ocean

N
W   E
S

South America's Population

Four big cities

Three-quarters of South America's population live in large, modern cities along the coast. There, bustling ports and harbors provide many people with jobs. Most of the continent's goods still arrive and leave by sea.

Farming the country

Only one-fourth of all South Americans live in the countryside. Most are poor and work on small farms. Life for these people has changed little over hundreds of years. In some places, small farms lie next to huge ranches owned by wealthy landowners.

Poor in the city

South America has a large number of people who are poor. Many of the poor live in shantytowns (*favelas*) built of wood, tin, and cardboard. The favelas on the hillsides of Rio de Janeiro are some of the best known.

Keeping with tradition

Native Americans make up more than half of Bolivia's population. Many still wear traditional ponchos, shawls, and round, felt hats.

The capital of Venezuela, **Caracas**, is one of the richest cities in South America. Most of the land around the city is used for mining and oil drilling.

Caracas, Venezuela

São Paulo, Brazil, has the largest population in South America. It borders a rich farming and industrial region.

The city of **Buenos Aires** lies on the coast of Argentina. Nearly 13 million people live there. It is the second-largest city on the continent.

Buenos Aires, Argentina

The Bolivian city of **La Paz** is one of the highest cities in the world. It is often called "the city that touches the clouds." La Paz is home to a large number of Native Americans.

- Few people, except Native Americans, live in the South American rain forests. It is too hot and humid.
- Because of the cold, oxygen-poor air, few people live in the high mountains.

People per Square Mile

- **place of interest**
- —— country boundary

| less than 5 | 5-25 | 25-125 | 125-250 | more than 250 |

Caracas
VENEZUELA

Equator

BRAZIL

BOLIVIA
La Paz

Pacific Ocean

São Paulo • • Rio de Janeiro

ARGENTINA

Buenos Aires

Atlantic Ocean

N
W E
S

In recent years, many people who once farmed in the mountains in northwestern South America have moved down to the coast to find better-paying jobs.

Farmland on a mountain slope in northwestern South America

DID YOU KNOW? Brazil has a very young population. Almost half of the people who live there are under 20 years old.

33

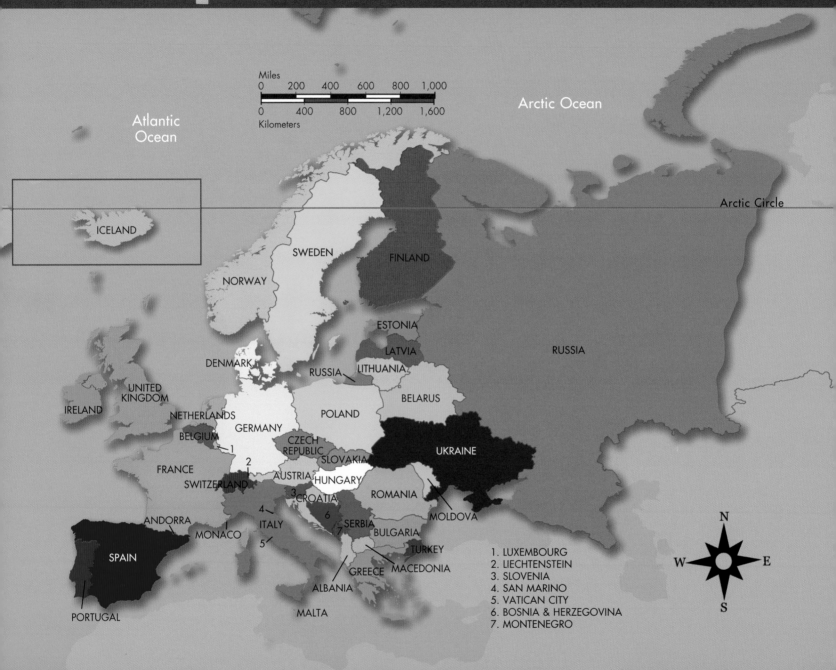

Miles
0 200 400 600 800 1,000

0 400 800 1,200 1,600
Kilometers

Atlantic Ocean

Arctic Ocean

Arctic Circle

ICELAND

SWEDEN

FINLAND

NORWAY

ESTONIA

LATVIA

LITHUANIA

DENMARK

RUSSIA

RUSSIA

BELARUS

UNITED KINGDOM

IRELAND

POLAND

NETHERLANDS

GERMANY

BELGIUM

CZECH REPUBLIC

SLOVAKIA

UKRAINE

FRANCE

AUSTRIA

HUNGARY

SWITZERLAND

CROATIA

ROMANIA

MOLDOVA

ANDORRA

ITALY

SERBIA

BULGARIA

MONACO

SPAIN

GREECE

MACEDONIA

TURKEY

ALBANIA

PORTUGAL

MALTA

1. LUXEMBOURG
2. LIECHTENSTEIN
3. SLOVENIA
4. SAN MARINO
5. VATICAN CITY
6. BOSNIA & HERZEGOVINA
7. MONTENEGRO

N
W   E
S

ALBANIA

ANDORRA

AUSTRIA

BELARUS

BELGIUM

BOSNIA & HERZEGOVINA

BULGARIA

CROATIA   CZECH REPUBLIC

DENMARK · ESTONIA · FINLAND · FRANCE

GERMANY · GREECE · HUNGARY · ICELAND

IRELAND · ITALY · LATVIA · LIECHTENSTEIN

LITHUANIA · LUXEMBOURG · MACEDONIA · MALTA

MOLDOVA · MONACO · MONTENEGRO · NETHERLANDS

NORWAY · POLAND · PORTUGAL · ROMANIA

RUSSIA · SAN MARINO · SERBIA · SLOVAKIA

SLOVENIA · SPAIN · SWEDEN · SWITZERLAND

TURKEY · UKRAINE · UNITED KINGDOM · VATICAN CITY

Continent size: the second-smallest of Earth's seven continents

Number of countries: 45; Russia and Turkey lie in two continents—Europe and Asia

Major languages: English, French, German, Greek, Hungarian

Total population: 732 million (2009 estimate)

Largest country (land size): Russia

Most populated country: Russia

Most populated city: Moscow, Russia

Climate: mostly mild in the West and continental (wet, warm to hot summers and cold winters) in the East; dry and cold all year in the far North; dry in the southeastern and southwestern regions; cool to cold in the mountains

Highest point: Mount Elbrus, Russia, 18,619 feet (5,679 meters)

Lowest point: northern shore of the Caspian Sea, 92 feet (28 m) below sea level

Longest river: Volga River

Largest body of water: Caspian Sea

Largest desert: Europe is the only continent with no deserts

Major agricultural products: barley, beans, citrus, fruits, corn, dairy products, goats, grapes, oats, olives

Major industries: agriculture, forestry, fishing, mining, manufacturing (clothing, iron, steel, ships, motor vehicles, railroad equipment, chemicals, and electronic equipment)

Natural resources: bauxite, coal, copper, iron ore, manganese

Europe's Landforms

Europe has many different types of landforms, including plateaus, plains, highlands, and many mountain ranges.

Along Europe's eastern border lie the great Ural Mountains. They divide Europe from Asia. Other high mountain ranges, such as the Alps, the Pyrenees, and the Caucasus, create natural borders between countries.

A smoking mountain

Mount Etna, on the Italian island of Sicily, is the tallest active volcano in Europe. A volcano is a type of mountain. It throws smoke, ash, and red-hot lava high into the air.

Mount Etna erupts on the island of Sicily, Italy.

Low-lying land

Most of the land in the Netherlands is below sea level. Long canals drain water from the flat, low-lying land. Without the canals, the land would be flooded by rain.

Northern European Plain

The Northern European Plain is one of the largest plains in the world. It stretches from the Pyrenees Mountains on the France-Spain border, across northern Europe, to the Ural Mountains of Russia. The land is mostly flat, with some hilly areas, including the Central Russian Uplands.

The Meseta

A huge plateau called the Meseta lies in the heart of Spain. Its average elevation (height) is 2,000 feet (610 meters) above sea level. The high, dry land of the Meseta covers about 40 percent of the Iberian Peninsula.

- The Kjolen Mountains of northern Europe are about half as tall as the Alps.
- Russia's Mount Elbrus is the highest mountain peak in Europe.
- The Caucasus Mountains form a bridge between the Black Sea and the Caspian Sea.
- The Italian peninsula is shaped like a boot.

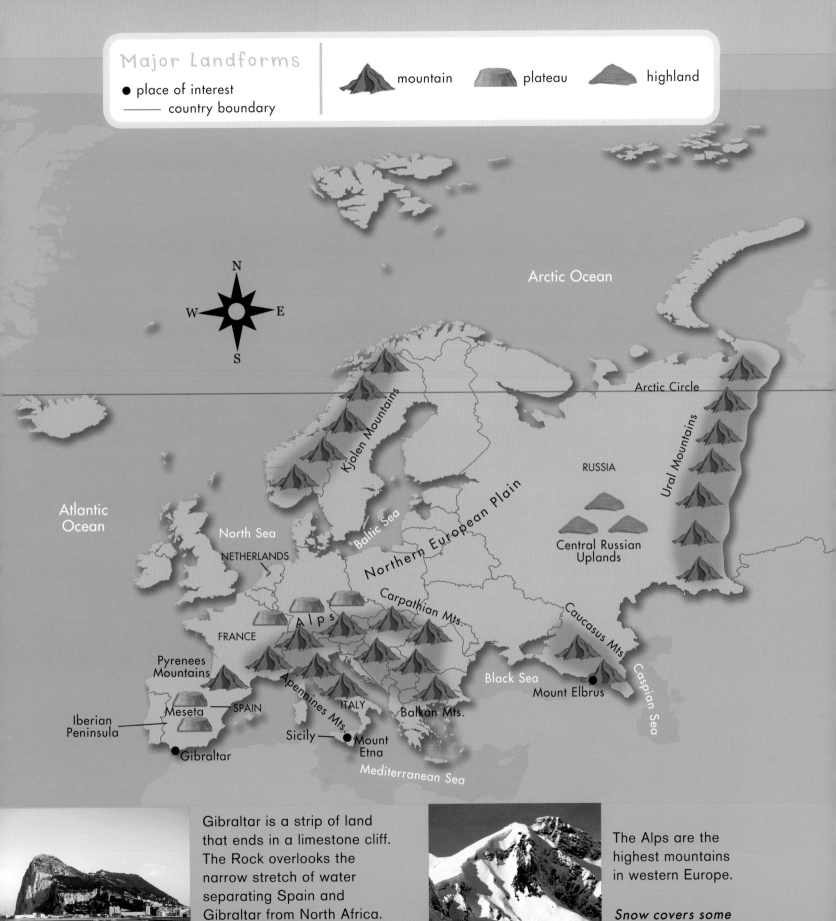

N
W E
S

Arctic Ocean

Arctic Circle

Kjolen Mountains

RUSSIA

Ural Mountains

Atlantic Ocean

North Sea

NETHERLANDS

Baltic Sea

Northern European Plain

Carpathian Mts.

Central Russian Uplands

A l p s

FRANCE

Pyrenees Mountains

Apennines Mts.

ITALY

Balkan Mts.

Caucasus Mts

Black Sea

Mount Elbrus

Caspian Sea

Iberian Peninsula

Meseta — SPAIN

Sicily —

Mount Etna

Gibraltar

Mediterranean Sea

Gibraltar is a strip of land that ends in a limestone cliff. The Rock overlooks the narrow stretch of water separating Spain and Gibraltar from North Africa.

The Rock of Gibraltar

The Alps are the highest mountains in western Europe.

Snow covers some of the Alps' peaks year-round.

37

Europe's Bodies of Water

Europe is bordered by two oceans: the Arctic Ocean to the north and the Atlantic Ocean to the west. It's bordered by five seas, as well: the North Sea, the Baltic Sea, the Mediterranean Sea, the Black Sea, and the Caspian Sea.

The continent also has many long rivers and thousands of lakes.

The Rhine River

The Rhine is a very long river. It flows from Switzerland, through Germany and the Netherlands, to the North Sea. It is one of the most important waterways in Europe. It is connected to other major rivers in Europe by man-made canals.

The Rhine River snakes past some of Germany's castles.

Fjords

Fjords are steep-sided, narrow waterways that stretch inland. These valleys were carved out of the rock by glaciers more than 10,000 years ago. When the ice melted, the sea level rose, and the valleys filled with water.

The fjords in western Norway are some of the most beautiful places in Europe.

Venice

Venice, Italy, is built on islands in the middle of a lagoon. A system of canals connects the islands.

Venetian boats called gondolas carry people around Venice.

- Finland has about 60,000 lakes, many with rocky islands in the middle.
- The Loire is France's longest river. It flows through rolling countryside and past large castles.

Major Bodies of Water

● place of interest ——— country boundary

⬤ lake 〰 river

N W E S

Arctic Ocean

Arctic Circle

Atlantic Ocean

North Sea

NORWAY

FINLAND

Lake Vanern

Lake Vattern

Baltic Sea

Lake Ladoga

Lake Onega

RUSSIA

Volga River

NETHERLANDS

Rotterdam ●

GERMANY

Oder River

Rhine River

Elbe River

Dnieper River

Don River

Thames River

Loire River

SWITZERLAND

FRANCE

Venice ●

Po River

ITALY

Danube River

Black Sea

Caspian Sea

Tagus River

Mediterranean Sea

• The salty Caspian Sea is the world's largest area of inland water.

• The Danube River flows through nine European countries. It connects the Black Sea with the industrial centers of western Europe and with the port of Rotterdam, Netherlands.

• The Volga is the longest river in Europe. It flows across Russia into the Caspian Sea. Many dams have been built across it, forming huge man-made lakes.

39

Europe's Climate

Although much of Europe lies closer to the Arctic Circle than to the equator, the continent's climate is fairly warm.

The reason is that the seas around Europe's coasts are warmed by special ocean currents.

Climate is the average weather a place has from season to season, year to year. Rainfall and temperature play large parts in a region's climate.

Land of the Midnight Sun

Part of Sweden lies north of the Arctic Circle. This area is called the Land of the Midnight Sun. The sun shines almost 24 hours a day there in late June and early July. In December and January, however, the sky is dark all day, and temperatures turn very cold.

A time-lapse photo of the midnight sun over northern Sweden in the summer

Mediterranean warmth

Countries around the Mediterranean Sea enjoy hot, dry summers and warm, wet winters. Winds blowing from the south bring warmth from the equator. Inland seas, such as the Mediterranean, also trap warmth from the sun. The seas stay warm because there are no strong ocean waves to cool them.

The warm waters of the Mediterranean coast

Climate basics

A region's climate depends upon three major things: how close it is to the ocean, how high up it is, and how close it is to the equator. Areas along the ocean have milder climates than areas farther inland. The higher a region is, and the farther it is from the equator, the colder its temperature.

- In Belgium, it rains an average of 208 days per year.
- Most of Norway's coastline lies near or within the Arctic Circle. But much of it has no ice or snow, even in the winter. Warm ocean winds keep ice and snow from forming.

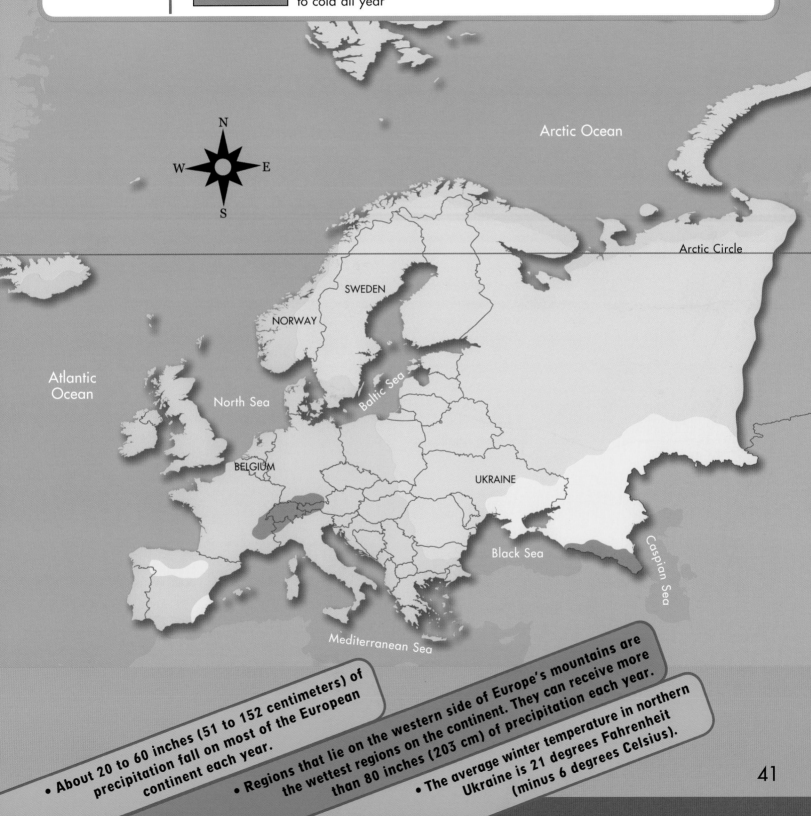

Climate

dry	dry most or all year with hot summers and warm to cold winters
polar	dry and cold all year
mountain	wet and dry seasons, cool to cold all year
mild	wet winters or all year with warm to hot summers and cool winters
continental	wet, warm to hot summers and cold winters

_____ country boundary

Arctic Ocean

N
W E
S

Arctic Circle

SWEDEN

NORWAY

Atlantic Ocean

North Sea

Baltic Sea

BELGIUM

UKRAINE

Black Sea

Caspian Sea

Mediterranean Sea

- About 20 to 60 inches (51 to 152 centimeters) of precipitation fall on most of the European continent each year.

- Regions that lie on the western side of Europe's mountains are the wettest regions on the continent. They can receive more than 80 inches (203 cm) of precipitation each year.

- The average winter temperature in northern Ukraine is 21 degrees Fahrenheit (minus 6 degrees Celsius).

Europe's Plants

Most plants on the European continent are well-adapted to the forest ecosystem. An ecosystem is all of the living and nonliving things in a certain area. It includes plants, animals, soil, weather ... everything!

On the grasslands of southeastern Europe, the soil is rich, but there aren't many trees. Tough grasses grow there. Wildflowers grow in the fields, forests, and mountain valleys of the milder West. Olive trees and vines grow best along the coasts of the warm Mediterranean Sea.

Some Plants of Europe

forest

	olive tree	The olive tree is native to the Mediterranean region. It can live for 500 years and grow back even after it has been chopped down.
	pine tree	Pine trees are a type of evergreen tree called a conifer. They have needle-like leaves and produce cones.
	tulip	Tulips come in every color except blue and true black. The Netherlands is well-known for growing tulips.
	wildflowers	The forests and grasslands of western Europe are carpeted with wildflowers. The United Kingdom has about 1,500 different wildflower species.

mountain

	gentian	The gentian is a very hardy flower that grows well in the cold mountain regions of Europe. Its blooms are usually blue or purple.

wetlands

	fern	Ferns grow well in dark, wet conditions. Their leaves are called fronds.
	cattails	Cattails are tall wetland plants with fuzzy, brown seed heads. Their stems and leaves provide shelter and food for many kinds of birds and fish.

tundra

	moss	Moss is one of the few plants hardy enough to survive the long, cold tundra winters.

42

Major Ecosystems

— country boundary

desert   grassland   mountain   wetlands

forest   ice cap   tundra

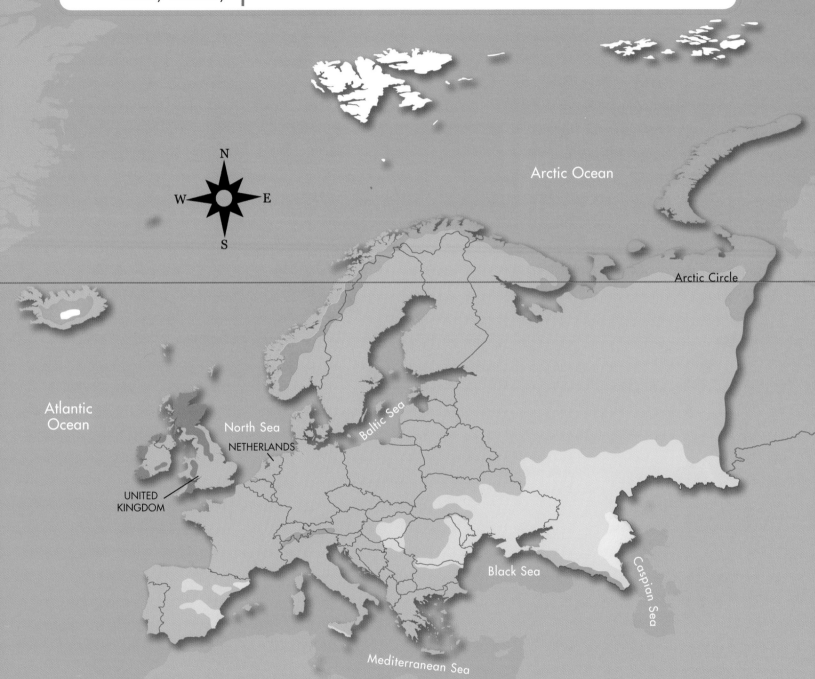

N
W   E
S

Arctic Ocean

Arctic Circle

Atlantic Ocean

North Sea

Baltic Sea

NETHERLANDS

UNITED KINGDOM

Black Sea

Caspian Sea

Mediterranean Sea

Europe's Animals

Although a variety of ecosystems exist in Europe, the forest ecosystem is the largest. An ecosystem is all of the living and nonliving things in a certain area.

Small animals such as rabbits, foxes, and badgers live in the forests of western Europe. Pine martens and wolverines live in the North. Wild boars and lynxs are two of the larger animals living in the forests of eastern Europe.

Some Animals of Europe

forest

deer	Deer feed on leaves and herbs and chew the bark of trees.
pine marten	The pine marten is a cat-sized animal with chestnut-brown fur, a creamy-yellow throat, and a long, bushy tail.
wild boar	The wild boar searches for roots just beneath the forest floor.
wolverine	The wolverine is a relative of the weasel. It's a shy animal, but it can be a fierce hunter.
bear	The brown bear lives in the forests of northeastern Europe. It feeds on berries, fish, and small animals.
gray wolf	Gray wolves live in the forests of northern and eastern Europe. They can also be found in tundra and mountain ecosystems.

mountain / tundra

golden eagle	When diving to catch its prey, the golden eagle can reach speeds of up to 200 miles (320 kilometers) an hour.
Iberian lynx	The Iberian lynx is a mountain cat found only in Europe. It leaps down on its prey from the trees.
ibex	The deer-like ibex climbs easily over rocky mountain slopes.
mountain hare	The mountain hare's brown summer fur turns mostly white in the winter. This change allows the hare to hide from predators in the snow.
reindeer	Both male and female reindeer have antlers. Antlers are shed (dropped) and regrown each year.

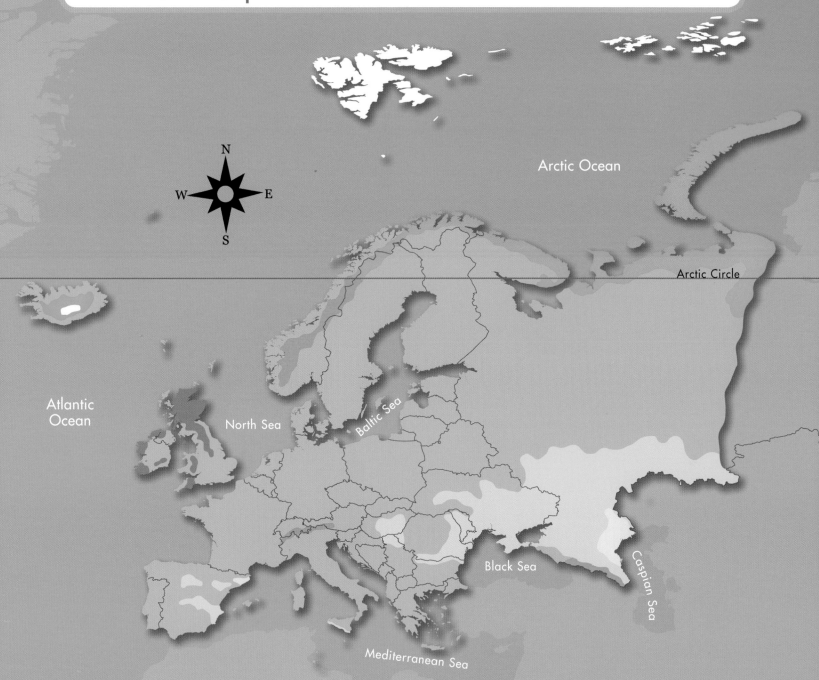

Major Ecosystems
—— country boundary

desert　　grassland　　mountain　　wetlands

forest　　ice cap　　tundra

N
W　E
S

Arctic Ocean

Arctic Circle

Atlantic Ocean

North Sea

Baltic Sea

Black Sea

Caspian Sea

Mediterranean Sea

Europe's Population

Compared to the other six continents, Europe is very crowded. It has the third-largest population, even though it is almost the smallest in land size.

People come to Europe's cities to work. As a result, Europe's population is large and growing quickly.

A European "family"

The European Union, or EU, is a group that was set up so European countries could trade easily with each other. Today, it is a growing "family" that works together to do more than just trade. More than half of all European countries belong to the EU. They use one common money system called the Euro.

Mountain villages

Few people live in Europe's mountain regions. Transportation is difficult, and the winters can be bitterly cold and snowy.

A village nestled in an Austrian mountain valley

Four big cities

Europe has some of the world's oldest and most famous cities. Tourists come from all over the world to visit its historical sites and museums.

London, United Kingdom, has nearly 7.5 million people. Many different cultures from all over the world make the city an exciting place to live.

Paris, France, has been a center of literature, art, and music for hundreds of years. More than 2 million people live in Paris, with another 10 million people living in the nearby suburbs.

One of Paris' most famous sites, the Eiffel Tower

Moscow is the capital of Russia, the country's most populated city, and the most populated city in Europe. About 11 million people live in Moscow.

The famous domes of St. Basil's Cathedral, a symbol of Moscow

With about 4 million people, **Berlin** is the most populated city in Germany. The German capital is famous for its festivals and nightlife.

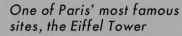

- For its size, Iceland is one of the world's least populated countries. It averages just seven people per square mile.
- Many people live along Italy's coasts because of the warm Mediterranean climate.
- The total population of Lithuania is 3.5 million people. This about the same number of people that live in the city of Berlin, Germany.

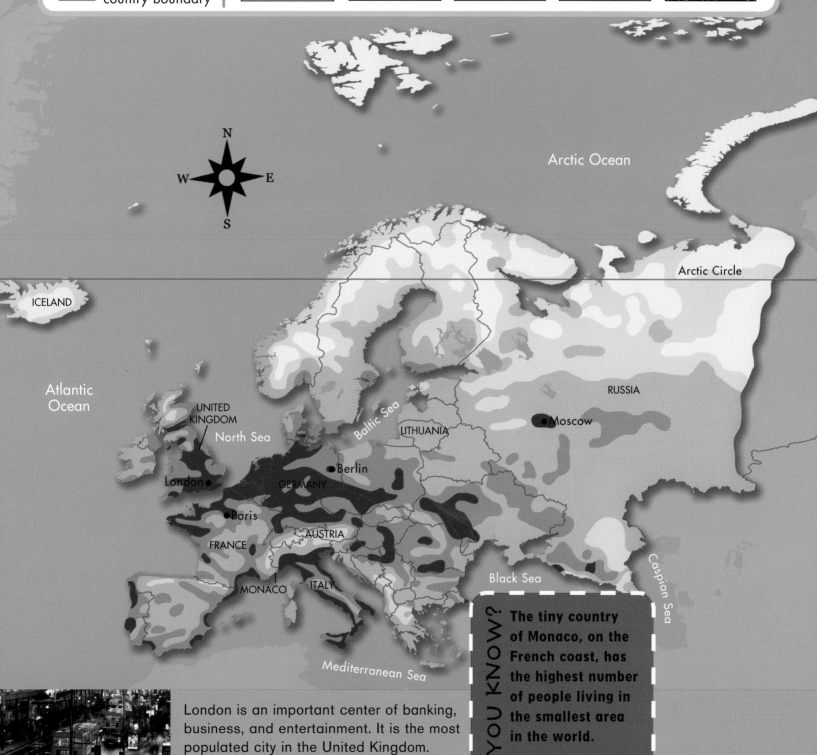

People per Square Mile

- ● place of interest
- —— country boundary

N
W E
S

Arctic Ocean

Arctic Circle

ICELAND

Atlantic Ocean

RUSSIA

●Moscow

UNITED KINGDOM

North Sea

Baltic Sea

LITHUANIA

London●

●Berlin

GERMANY

●Paris

AUSTRIA

FRANCE

Black Sea

Caspian Sea

MONACO   ITALY

Mediterranean Sea

London is an important center of banking, business, and entertainment. It is the most populated city in the United Kingdom.

London bustles with activity both day and night.

DID YOU KNOW? The tiny country of Monaco, on the French coast, has the highest number of people living in the smallest area in the world.

47

ALGERIA

ANGOLA

BENIN

BOTSWANA

BURKINA FASO

BURUNDI

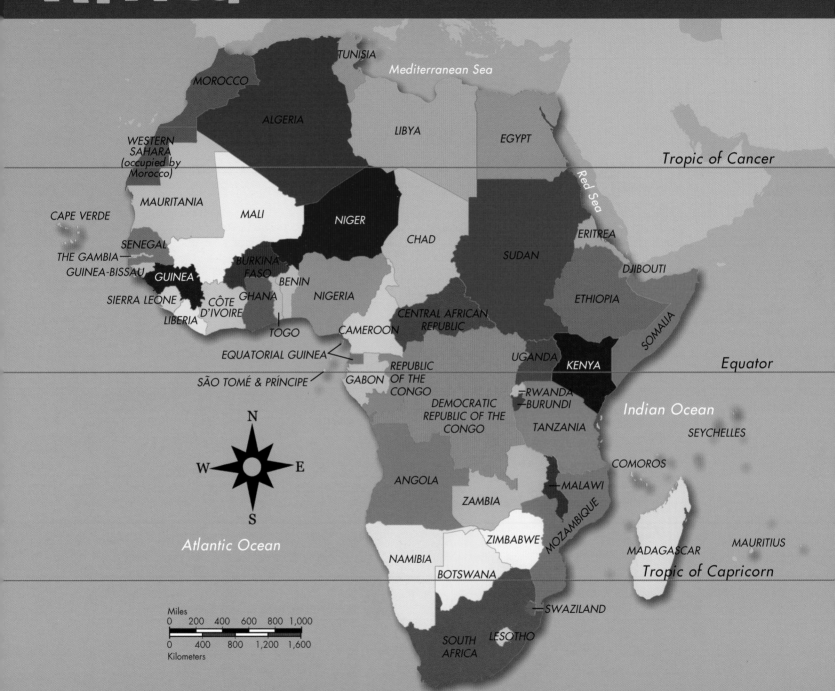

TUNISIA

Mediterranean Sea

MOROCCO

ALGERIA

LIBYA

EGYPT

Tropic of Cancer

WESTERN
SAHARA
(occupied by
Morocco)

MAURITANIA

MALI

NIGER

CHAD

Red Sea

SUDAN

ERITREA

DJIBOUTI

CAPE VERDE

SENEGAL

THE GAMBIA
GUINEA-BISSAU
GUINEA

BURKINA
FASO

BENIN

ETHIOPIA

SIERRA LEONE
CÔTE
D'IVOIRE
GHANA

NIGERIA

CENTRAL AFRICAN
REPUBLIC

SOMALIA

LIBERIA

TOGO

CAMEROON

EQUATORIAL GUINEA

SÃO TOMÉ & PRÍNCIPE

REPUBLIC
OF THE
CONGO

GABON

UGANDA

KENYA

Equator

RWANDA
BURUNDI

DEMOCRATIC
REPUBLIC OF THE
CONGO

TANZANIA

Indian Ocean

SEYCHELLES

N

COMOROS

W   E

ANGOLA

ZAMBIA

MALAWI

MOZAMBIQUE

S

Atlantic Ocean

ZIMBABWE

MADAGASCAR

MAURITIUS

NAMIBIA

BOTSWANA

Tropic of Capricorn

Miles
0   200 400 600 800 1,000

SWAZILAND

0   400   800   1,200 1,600
Kilometers

SOUTH
AFRICA

LESOTHO

CAMEROON

CAPE VERDE

CENTRAL AFRICAN
REPUBLIC

CHAD

COMOROS

DEMOCRATIC
REPUBLIC OF THE
CONGO

REPUBLIC OF
THE CONGO

CÔTE D'IVOIRE   DJIBOUTI   EGYPT   EQUATORIAL GUINEA

ERITREA   ETHIOPIA   GABON   THE GAMBIA

GHANA   GUINEA   GUINEA-BISSAU   KENYA

LESOTHO   LIBERIA   LIBYA   MADAGASCAR

MALAWI   MALI   MAURITANIA   MAURITIUS

MOROCCO   MOZAMBIQUE   NAMIBIA   NIGER

NIGERIA   RWANDA   SÃO TOMÉ & PRÍNCIPE   SENEGAL

SEYCHELLES   SIERRA LEONE   SOMALIA   SOUTH AFRICA

SUDAN   SWAZILAND   TANZANIA   TOGO

TUNISIA   UGANDA   ZAMBIA   ZIMBABWE

Continent size: the second-largest of Earth's seven continents

Number of countries: 53

Major languages: Arabic; English; French; Portuguese; more than 1,000 native African languages, including Swahili, Hausa, Yoruba, and Somali

Total population: 1 billion (2009 estimate)

Largest country (land size): Sudan

Most populated country: Nigeria

Most populated city: Cairo, Egypt

Climate: dry in the northern region, with hot summers and warm to cold winters; tropical in the central region; dry and mild in the southern region; cool to cold in the mountains

Highest point: Mount Kilimanjaro, Tanzania, 19,340 feet (5,899 meters)

Lowest point: Lake Asal, Djibouti, 502 feet (153 m) below sea level

Longest river: Nile River

Largest body of water: Lake Victoria

Largest desert: Sahara Desert

Major agricultural products: bananas, beef, cacao beans, cloves, coffee, corn

Major industries: mining, agriculture, oil manufacturing (consumer goods such as clothing, beverages, footwear, and soap)

Natural resources: bauxite, chromium, cobalt, diamonds, gold

Africa's Landforms

Africa has many different types of landforms, including mountains, plateaus, and valleys.

In northern Africa lies the world's largest desert, the Sahara. It is bordered by a band of semi-desert land called the Sahel.

Mount Kilimanjaro, Africa's tallest mountain, rises to the southeast. Most of the rest of the continent is high, flat plateau, broken by smaller mountains and ridges.

Shaping the land

In the Sahara Desert, strong winds and sandstorms form the rocks into interesting shapes.

Rock sculptures in the Sahara

The Great Rift Valley

The Great Rift Valley is a chain of steep-sided valleys in East Africa. It was formed millions of years ago by movements deep within the planet. The valley floor is not flat. It is dotted with hills. These hills are volcanoes. A volcano is a kind of mountain that can spew out lava, ashes, and hot gases from deep inside the earth. About 30 of them are still active.

The Great Rift Valley as seen from the air

The oldest desert

The Namib Desert is the oldest desert in the world. It is also huge. The word *namib* means "endless." The desert is known as a "dune sea." The winds constantly move and change the shape of the desert's large, wave-like dunes.

- The northern slopes of the Atlas Mountains receive a lot of rain and are covered with farmland and forests. The southern slopes are dry and grassy.
- The Horn of Africa is a curved peninsula that sticks out into the Red Sea.
- The Drakensberg Mountains stretch nearly 700 miles (1,120 kilometers) along Africa's southeastern coast.

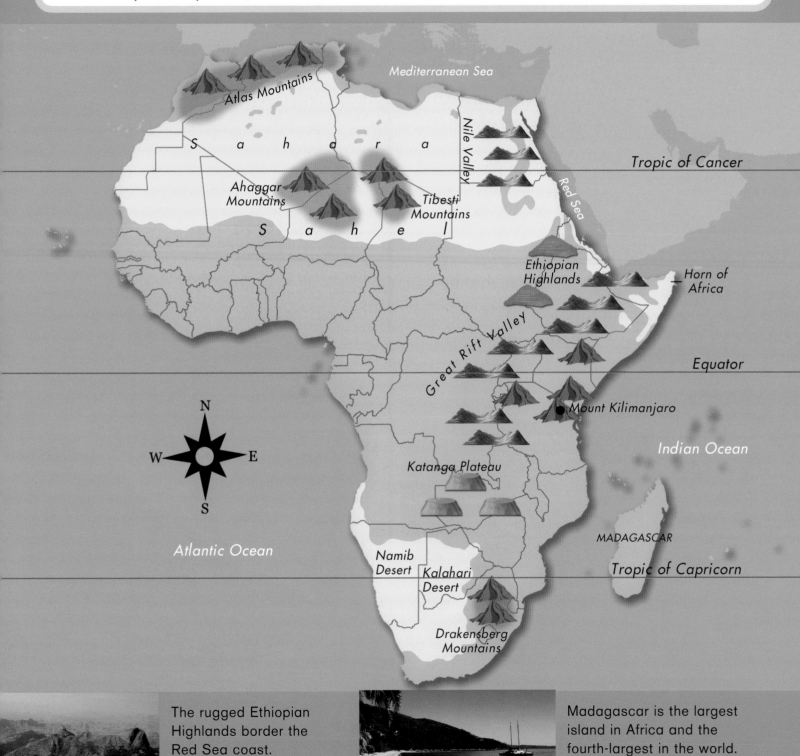

Major Landforms

● place of interest
—— country boundary

 mountain   plateau highland valley

Mediterranean Sea

Atlas Mountains

S a h a r a

Tropic of Cancer

Nile Valley

Red Sea

Ahaggar Mountains

Tibesti Mountains

S a h e l

Ethiopian Highlands

Horn of Africa

Great Rift Valley

Equator

● Mount Kilimanjaro

Indian Ocean

Katanga Plateau

N
W   E
S

MADAGASCAR

Atlantic Ocean

Namib Desert

Kalahari Desert

Tropic of Capricorn

Drakensberg Mountains

The rugged Ethiopian Highlands border the Red Sea coast.

A young goatherder grazes his goats in the Ethiopian Highlands.

Madagascar is the largest island in Africa and the fourth-largest in the world.

The beaches of eastern Madagascar drop sharply into deep water.

51

Africa's Bodies of Water

Africa has a lot of water. Four of its greatest rivers are the Nile, the Congo, the Niger, and the Zambezi.

Most of the continent's lakes are on its eastern side. There, chains of long, deep lakes have formed in the bottom of valleys.

The Okavango Delta in southern Africa and the Sudd in eastern Africa are dotted with lagoons.

Giant sponge

The Sudd is a giant wetland in Sudan. It acts as a sponge that soaks up the flood waters of the Nile River. Because the region is so hot, half of the Sudd's water evaporates (turns from a liquid into a gas) before it can drain away.

One of the Nile's tributaries, the White Nile, runs through the Sudd.

The Limpopo River

The slow-moving, muddy Limpopo River zigzags through South Africa on its way to the Indian Ocean. The river was made famous in the story "The Elephant's Child" by Rudyard Kipling. Kipling described the river as "the great gray-green, greasy Limpopo River, all set about with fever-trees."

The Victoria Falls

The Victoria Falls lie halfway down the Zambezi River. They are one of the world's largest waterfalls. Water crashes 360 feet (110 meters) over a cliff, causing a sound like thunder. Their African name is *Mosi-oa-Tunya*, meaning "smoke that thunders."

Spray from the crashing water of the Victoria Falls looks like smoke.

• The Nile is the longest river in the world. It begins in Rwanda and flows north to Egypt, where it drains into the Mediterranean Sea.

• The first non-African person to view Victoria Falls was a Scottish explorer named David Livingstone. He named the falls Victoria, after the then-Queen of England.

Major Bodies of Water

● place of interest — country boundary

🗿 lake 〰 river

Mediterranean Sea

EGYPT

Tropic of Cancer

Nile River

Red Sea

● Aswan High Dam

Blue Nile

Niger River

Lake Chad

SUDAN

— Lake Assal

White Nile

● The Sudd

— Lake Turkana

— Lake Albert

Congo River

— Lake Victoria

Equator

Indian Ocean

RWANDA —

— Lake Tanganyika

N
W · E
S

Okavango Delta ●

Zambezi River

— Lake Malawi

● Victoria Falls

Atlantic Ocean

Limpopo River

Tropic of Capricorn

Orange River

SOUTH AFRICA

Africa's Lake Victoria is the second-largest freshwater lake in the world. Lake Superior, in North America, is the largest.

Lake Victoria is about 255 miles (408 kilometers) long and 155 miles (155 km) wide.

DID YOU KNOW? Because of their beauty and life-giving water, the lakes of East Africa have been described as a "chain of sapphires." Sapphires are valuable, deep blue gemstones.

Africa's Climate

Most of Africa lies between the Tropic of Cancer and the Tropic of Capricorn. Because of this location, much of the continent has a dry or tropical climate.

Climate is the average weather a place has from season to season, year to year. Rainfall and temperature play large parts in a region's climate.

Lightning flashes through the trees during a tropical storm in Africa.

Seasons

In the regions that lie on either side of the equator, the climate is tropical (mountain regions have their own climate). It is always hot there, so instead of hot and cold seasons, the regions have wet and dry seasons. Rain often falls heavily just once or twice during the rainy season, bringing storms and floods.

Hot winds

Strong, hot winds blow across the dry desert regions of northern Africa. Different types of winds have different names, depending upon when and where they blow. Very strong winds can form sandstorms that last for hours or even days.

Sandstorms fill the sky with sand, blocking out the sun.

Climate basics

A region's climate depends upon three major things: how close it is to the ocean, how high up it is, and how close it is to the equator. Areas along the ocean have milder climates than areas farther inland. The higher a region is, and the farther it is from the equator, the colder its temperature.

- The hottest temperature on Earth was recorded in Al Aziziyah, Libya, in September 1922. It was 136 degrees Fahrenheit (58 degrees Celsius).
- Less than 10 inches (25 centimeters) of rain fall each year in Africa's dry climate regions.
- Africa's tallest mountain regions have a cool climate because they are so high above sea level.

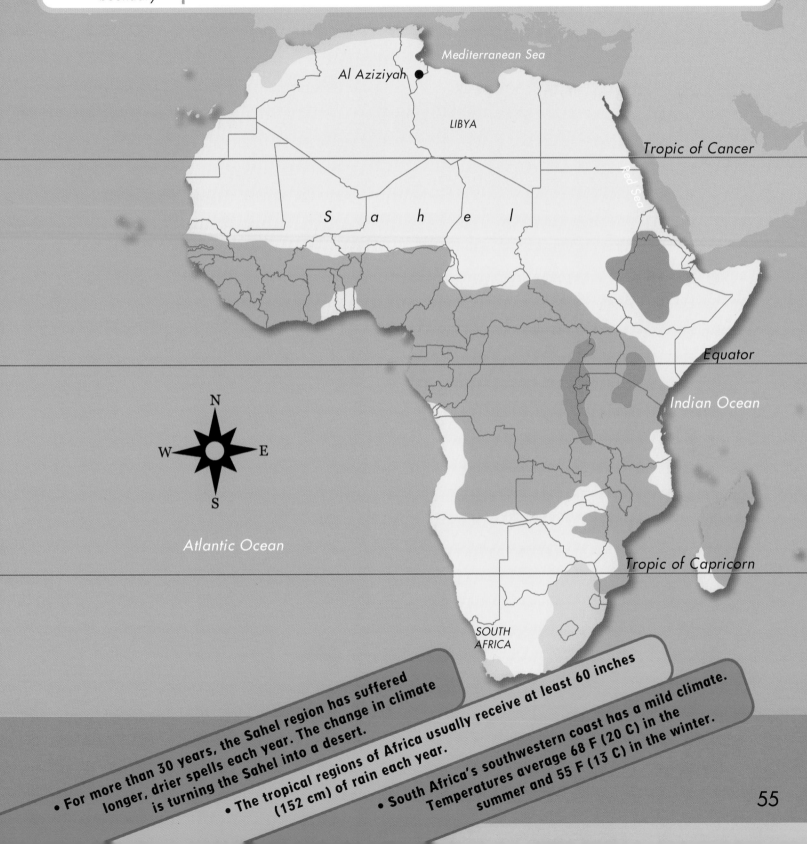

Climate

- ● place of interest
- —— country boundary

dry	dry most or all year with hot summers and warm to cold winters
mild	wet winters or all year with warm to hot summers and cool winters
tropical	wet and dry seasons, hot all year
mountain	wet and dry seasons, cool to cold all year

Mediterranean Sea

Al Aziziyah ●

LIBYA

Tropic of Cancer

Red Sea

S a h e l

Equator

Indian Ocean

N
W   E
S

Atlantic Ocean

Tropic of Capricorn

SOUTH
AFRICA

- For more than 30 years, the Sahel region has suffered longer, drier spells each year. The change in climate is turning the Sahel into a desert.

- The tropical regions of Africa usually receive at least 60 inches (152 cm) of rain each year.

- South Africa's southwestern coast has a mild climate. Temperatures average 68 F (20 C) in the summer and 55 F (13 C) in the winter.

55

Africa's Plants

Desert and grassland ecosystems cover much of the African continent. An ecosystem is all of the living and nonliving things in a certain area. It includes plants, animals, soil, weather ... everything!

Many African plants have adapted to dry, warm conditions. Trees such as the date palm and the baobab store water in their trunks. Flowers and grasses on the tropical grassland (also called the savanna) have long roots that reach water deep underground.

Some Plants of Africa

desert	date palm	The fruits of the date palm, called dates, grow in large clumps that hang down from the tree.
forest	ebony tree	The wood of the ebony tree is black, heavy, and very hard.
grassland	acacia tree	The flat-topped acacia tree grows on the hot, dry grasslands. Its juicy leaves provide food for many animals, such as giraffes.
grassland	baobab	Baobabs store water in their huge trunks. The trees' star-shaped flowers smell sweet.
grassland	fireball lily	Blood-red fireball lilies produce just one flowerhead each season. The flowerhead may measure up to 10 inches (25 centimeters) across and contain 200 flowers.

rain forest	fern	Ferns grow well on the dark, damp floor of the rain forest.
rain forest	liana	The liana is a creeping vine that grows on trees. It climbs to the treetops, where it bursts into flower.
rain forest	orchid	Orchids are the largest family of plants in the world. Their flowers come in many different shapes and colors.
wetlands	mangrove tree	Mangrove trees grow in saltwater swamps along the shoreline and on riverbanks. Their long, twisted roots look like stilts.
wetlands	papyrus	The papyrus plant, with its tufted heads, grows in the wetlands of northeastern Africa and the Okavango Delta farther south.

56

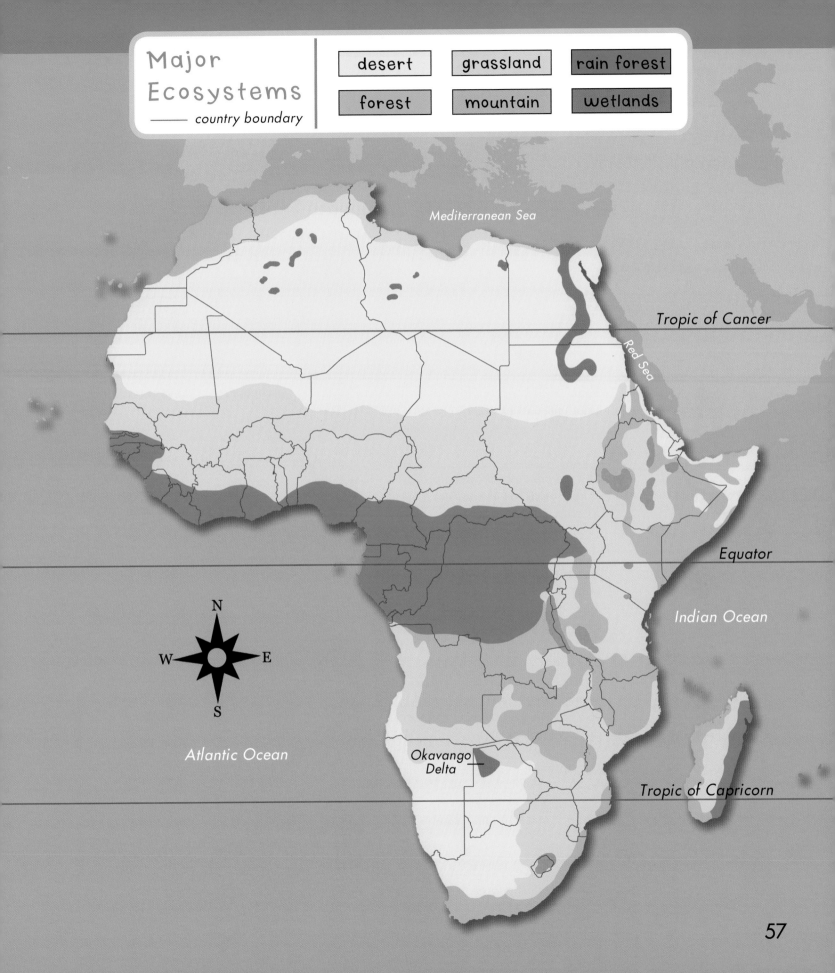

Major Ecosystems
— country boundary

desert grassland rain forest
forest mountain wetlands

Mediterranean Sea

Tropic of Cancer

Red Sea

N
W   E
S

Equator

Indian Ocean

Atlantic Ocean

Okavango
Delta

Tropic of Capricorn

57

Africa's Animals

Africa is home to a variety of animals. Many are well-adapted to the continent's desert and grassland ecosystems. An ecosystem is all of the living and nonliving things in a certain area.

Herds of zebras and other grazing animals, as well as meat-eating lions and cheetahs, live on the grasslands. Hippos feed on river plants, while monkeys and gorillas eat fruits and leaves in the steamy rain forest.

Some Animals of Africa

desert

camel	The camel stores food in its hump and can survive on small amounts of water.
scorpion	The scorpion uses the deadly stinger on its tail to paralyze its prey.
viper	The saw-scaled viper rubs parts of its body together to make a sound that frightens away its enemies.

rain forest

gorilla	Although leaves and fruit make up most of their diet, gorillas also eat insects such as termites and caterpillars.
ringtailed lemur	The ringtailed lemur lives only on the island of Madagascar.
mandrill	The mandrill is a large monkey found only in Africa. It has thick blue and purple ridges alongside its bright-red nose.

grassland

cheetah	The cheetah is the fastest land animal. It can catch its prey in less than a minute.
impala	Impalas are light on their feet. They jump up and race for cover when wild cats come near.
zebra	Zebras have striped coats that help them stay hidden behind trees and bushes.
lion	Lions live in groups called prides. Up to 40 lions may live in a pride.
hippopotamus	The hippopotamus (hippo) is the second-heaviest land mammal (after the elephant).
wildebeest	Wildebeest travel hundreds of miles each year in search of grass and water.
giraffe	Found only on the African grasslands, giraffes are the tallest land animals.

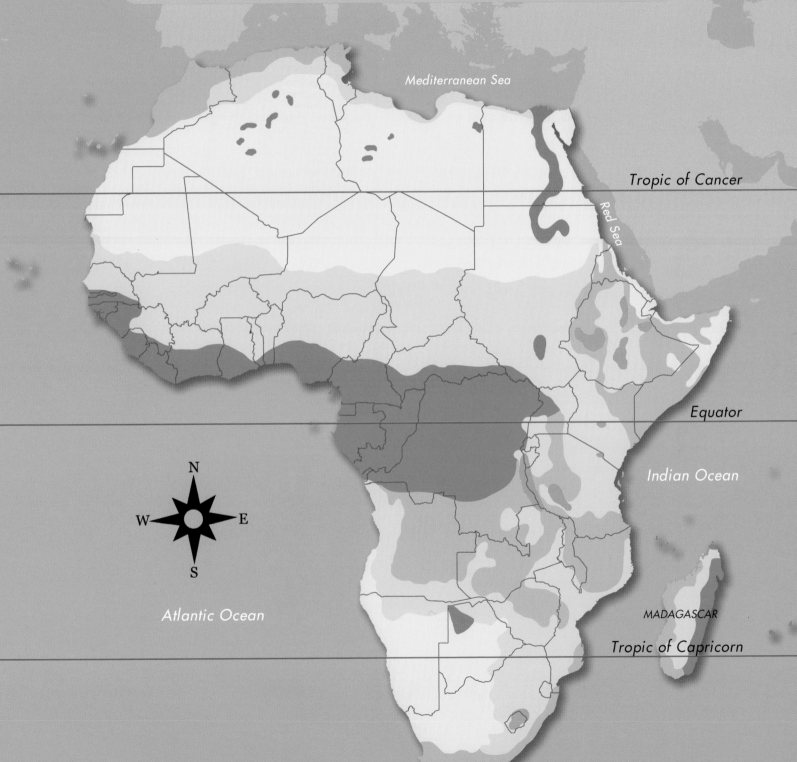

Major Ecosystems
— country boundary

desert   grassland   rain forest
forest   mountain   wetlands

Mediterranean Sea

Tropic of Cancer

Red Sea

Equator

Indian Ocean

N
W — E
S

Atlantic Ocean

MADAGASCAR

Tropic of Capricorn

Africa's Population

Big cities

There are more than 50 African cities with populations greater than 1 million, including Algiers, Algeria; Casablanca, Morocco; and Cape Town, South Africa.

Africa is a continent of young people. Almost half of the population is under 15 years of age. The population in Africa is growing faster than any other continent's population.

Many Africans live in big, bustling cities. Others live in small villages where people must walk for miles to get water.

Nairobi, Kenya

Nairobi is the capital of Kenya. With about 3 million people, it's also a large business center. Modern office buildings and hotels are set on wide, tree-lined streets.

The Nigerian city of **Lagos** is growing amazingly fast. Now Africa's second-most populated city, Lagos is soon expected to be one of the world's top five biggest cities.

Lagos, Nigeria

Health and disease

Food shortages and life-threatening diseases such as cholera, malaria, and HIV/AIDS are common in many parts of Africa. Good health care is not available for all Africans. As a result, people in many African countries cannot expect to live long lives. In Niger, for example, the average life expectancy is 44. In Malawi, it's only 43.

Cairo, Egypt

Cairo, the capital of Egypt, is the most populated city in Africa. More than 10 million people live there. Many of them live in crowded, run-down housing.

- Nigeria has more people than any other country in Africa.
- Namibia averages just five people per square mile.
- Many people live in the Great Lakes region (Burundi, Kenya, Rwanda, Tanzania, and Uganda). It has some of Africa's best farmland, which provides jobs and food.

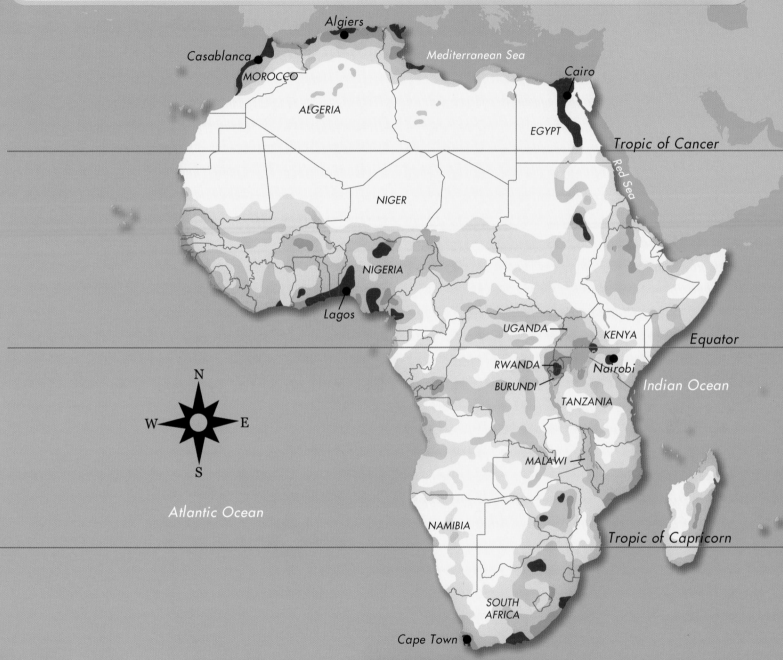

People per Square Mile

- ● place of interest
- —— country boundary

less than 5	5-25	25-125	125-250	more than 250

Algiers

Casablanca

MOROCCO

Mediterranean Sea

Cairo

ALGERIA

EGYPT

Tropic of Cancer

Red Sea

NIGER

NIGERIA

Lagos

UGANDA

KENYA

Equator

RWANDA

Nairobi

BURUNDI

Indian Ocean

TANZANIA

N
W E
S

MALAWI

Atlantic Ocean

NAMIBIA

Tropic of Capricorn

SOUTH AFRICA

Cape Town

People often live around green oases on the edges of the African deserts.

An oasis in northwestern Africa

The Zulu people of Africa have the largest population of any African group. In the 19th century, their kingdom covered most of South Africa.

Zulu tribespeople

61

Arctic Ocean

Arctic Circle

RUSSIA

Pacific Ocean

KAZAKHSTAN

UZBEKISTAN

GEORGIA

KYRGYZSTAN

TURKMENISTAN

1. ARMENIA
2. AZERBAIJAN
3. CYPRUS
4. LEBANON
5. BAHRAIN
6. QATAR
7. UNITED ARAB EMIRATES

TURKEY

1

2

TAJIKISTAN

3

SYRIA

IRAN

AFGHANISTAN

4

IRAQ

NEPAL

BHUTAN

ISRAEL

KUWAIT

JORDAN

5

PAKISTAN

Tropic of Cancer

6

SAUDI ARABIA

7

OMAN

INDIA

BANGLADESH

YEMEN

N

W   E

S

Miles
0 200 400 600 800 1,000

0   400 800 1,200 1,600
Kilometers

SRI LANKA

MALDIVES

Equator

Indian Ocean

AFGHANISTAN　ARMENIA　AZERBAIJAN　BAHRAIN

BANGLADESH　BHUTAN　CYPRUS　GEORGIA

INDIA　IRAN　IRAQ　ISRAEL

JORDAN　KAZAKHSTAN　KUWAIT　KYRGYZSTAN

LEBANON　MALDIVES　NEPAL　OMAN

PAKISTAN　QATAR　RUSSIA　SAUDI ARABIA

SRI LANKA　SYRIA　TAJIKISTAN　TURKEY

TURKMENISTAN　UNITED ARAB EMIRATES　UZBEKISTAN　YEMEN

Continent size: Asia, as a whole, is the largest of Earth's seven continents

Number of countries: 32 in the region, 49 total in Asia; Russia and Turkey lie in two continents—Europe and Asia

Major languages: Arabic, Bengali, English, Greek, Hebrew

Total population: 2 billion (2009 estimate)

Largest country (land size): Russia

Most populated country: India

Most populated city: Mumbai, India

Climate: mostly dry in Southwest Asia, with a mild climate around the Black Sea and the Mediterranean Sea; continental (wet, warm to hot summers and cold winters) in the East; dry and cold all year in the far North; dry in the southeastern and southwestern regions; cool to cold in the mountains

Highest point: Mount Everest, Nepal/China, 29,035 feet (8,856 meters)

Lowest point: Dead Sea, Israel/Jordan, 1,349 feet (411 m) below sea level

Longest river: Ob-Irtysh River

Largest body of water: Caspian Sea

Largest desert: Rub' al Khali Desert

Major agricultural products: citrus fruits, cotton, dates, goats, grapes, jute

Major industries: agriculture, construction, mining, manufacturing (clothing, chemicals, food and beverage, cement, steel, and electronic equipment)

Natural resources: aluminum, coal, copper, gold, natural gas

Southwest and Central Asia's Landforms

Much of Southwest and Central Asia is rugged and covered with mountains, plateaus, and highlands. The world's tallest mountains lie in this region.

But the region also has one of the world's largest stretches of low, flat land. The West Siberian Plain covers about one-third of Siberia. Siberia is the part of Russia that lies east of the Ural Mountains.

A lot of sand

The Rub' al Khali Desert is also known as the Empty Quarter. Deserts are not landforms, but the Rub' al Khali is an important part of Southwest Asia's landscape. It stretches across one-third of the Arabian Peninsula and is one of the largest sand deserts in the world.

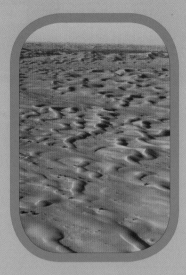

The bare, sandy Rub' al Khali is very valuable land because it holds the world's largest amounts of oil.

The Himalayas

The Himalayas are the tallest mountains in the world. The mountain range was formed over millions of years and is still growing. The highest peak is Mount Everest. It stands 29,035 feet (8,856 meters) tall.

A view of the Himalayas

The salt swamp of Iran

In northern Iran lies a large, desert-like salt swamp called the Dasht-e Kavir. No one lives in this area. The ground is a lot like quicksand and is very dangerous to walk on.

The salty crust of Iran's Dasht-e Kavir

- Nearly all of Tajikistan—93 percent—is covered with mountains.
- The Ural Mountains form part of the boundary between Europe and Asia.
- The Deccan is a large plateau in India that covers most of the central and southern parts of the country.

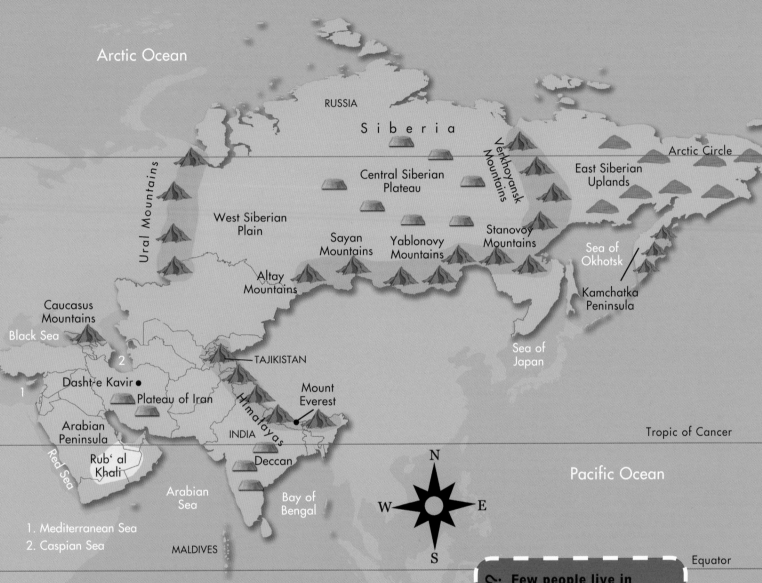

Arctic Ocean

RUSSIA

S i b e r i a

Verkhoyansk Mountains

Central Siberian Plateau

Arctic Circle

East Siberian Uplands

Ural Mountains

West Siberian Plain

Sayan Mountains

Yablonovy Mountains

Stanovoy Mountains

Sea of Okhotsk

Altay Mountains

Kamchatka Peninsula

Caucasus Mountains

Black Sea

Sea of Japan

2

TAJIKISTAN

1

Dasht-e Kavir ●

Plateau of Iran

Himalayas

Mount Everest

Tropic of Cancer

Arabian Peninsula

INDIA

Pacific Ocean

Red Sea

Rub' al Khali

Deccan

N

Arabian Sea

Bay of Bengal

W   E

1. Mediterranean Sea
2. Caspian Sea

MALDIVES

S

Equator

Indian Ocean

The Maldives are a group of islands called atolls. An atoll is the tip of an extinct (dead) volcano that rises from the bottom of the ocean.

One of many atolls in the Maldives

DID YOU KNOW? Few people live in Siberia because much of the area is covered with tall mountains and plateaus. Siberia even has volcanoes, on the Kamchatka Peninsula. A volcano is a type of mountain. It throws smoke, ash, and red-hot lava high into the air.

65

Southwest and Central Asia's
Bodies of Water

Many rivers flow across Southwest and Central Asia. Three large, salty inland seas (the Aral Sea, the Caspian Sea, and the Dead Sea) also lie within the region.

Southwest and Central Asia share their borders with three oceans: the Arctic Ocean, the Pacific Ocean, and the Indian Ocean.

Dry riverbeds

A wadi is a dry riverbed. It contains water only during times of heavy rain. People in desert countries often live in wadis because there is always water just below the surface. However, wadis can be dangerous. When it rains, they flood suddenly, which can catch people off-guard.

When the rains come, this dry wadi may suddenly flood.

The Dead Sea

The Dead Sea is a very salty body of water in Southwest Asia. It is also the lowest point on Earth, lying 1,349 feet (411 meters) below sea level. The salt makes it possible for people to float easily on the water.

A swimmer floating on the Dead Sea

The Ganges River

The Ganges River is one of the world's most important rivers. It flows 1,557 miles (2,491 kilometers) from northeastern India to the Bay of Bengal. The Ganges is a holy river for followers of a religion called Hinduism. Hindus believe the Ganges is a goddess who forgives all sins and helps the dead reach heaven.

- Lake Baikal, in Central Asia, is the oldest, deepest freshwater lake on Earth. More than 330 rivers and streams flow into it. The lake's surface freezes for five or six months each year.

- The Aral Sea is turning into a desert. It has lost almost 75 percent of its water since 1960. Much of the water from incoming rivers is used for crops, cutting off the sea's water supply.

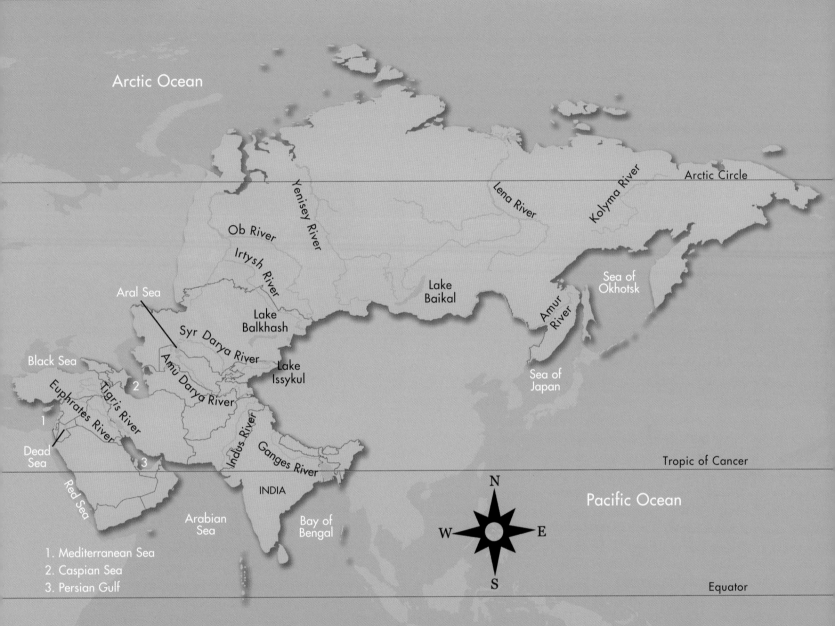

Major Bodies of Water

—— country boundary   🔵 lake   〰 river

Arctic Ocean

Arctic Circle

Yenisey River

Ob River

Lena River

Kolyma River

Irtysh River

Aral Sea

Lake Baikal

Sea of Okhotsk

Syr Darya River

Lake Balkhash

Amu Darya River

Amur River

Black Sea

2

Lake Issykul

Tigris River

Euphrates River

Sea of Japan

1

Dead Sea

3

Indus River

Ganges River

Tropic of Cancer

Red Sea

INDIA

Pacific Ocean

Arabian Sea

Bay of Bengal

N
W   E
S

1. Mediterranean Sea
2. Caspian Sea
3. Persian Gulf

Equator

Indian Ocean

Lake Issykul is a huge lake. It lies in the crater of an old volcano. Water from melted snow in the nearby mountains feeds the lake. The water is so clear that you can see objects 40 feet (12 m) below the surface.

Lake Issykul is surrounded by mountains.

67

Southwest and Central Asia's
Climate

Climate is the average weather a place has from season to season, year to year. Rainfall and temperature play large parts in a region's climate.

Because the Southwest and Central Asia region stretches from above the Arctic Circle to the equator, it has a very wide range of climates.

Northernmost places have a polar climate, while southernmost places have a tropical climate.

In the Tropics

India, Bangladesh, and Sri Lanka lie in the Tropics. The climate is hot, but the countries' shores are cooled by ocean breezes. There is heavy rainfall when the monsoon winds blow in from the Indian Ocean.

A tropical beach in Sri Lanka

Mountain climate

High up in the tallest mountains of Southwest and Central Asia, it is cold all year. The snow and ice never melt. Ice fields form from snow that has become pressed and frozen into ice. In places, this pressing forms sharp "knives" of ice, like icicles pointing upward.

An ice field high in the mountains of Southwest Asia

Climate basics

A region's climate depends upon three major things: how close it is to the ocean, how high up it is, and how close it is to the equator. Areas along the ocean have milder climates than areas farther inland. The higher a region is, and the farther it is from the equator, the colder its temperature.

• June through September is the monsoon season in Southwest Asia. Places along the Indian Ocean may receive from 20 to 80 inches (51 to 203 centimeters) of rain during this time.

• In the far northern part of the continent, north of the Arctic Circle, the summer season lasts about a month. During this time, daylight can last almost 24 hours.

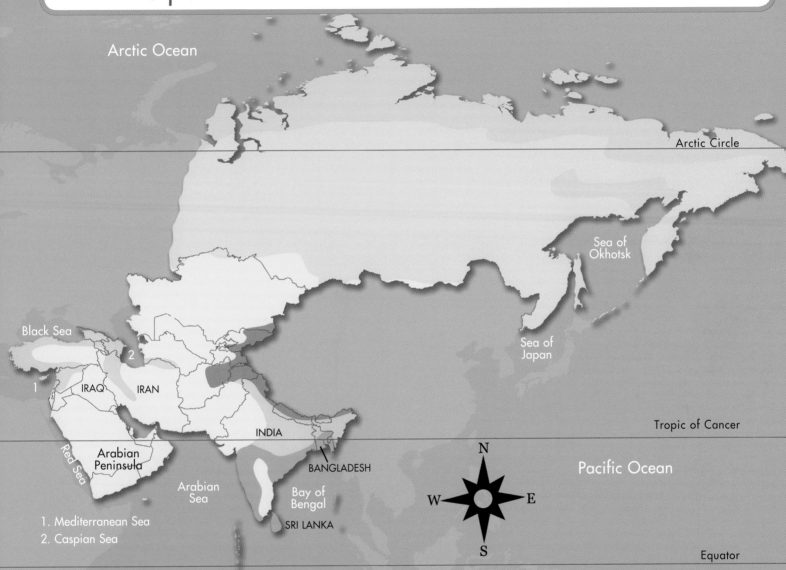

Climate

dry	dry most or all year with hot summers and warm to cold winters
polar	dry and cold all year
mountain	wet and dry seasons, cool to cold all year
mild	wet winters or all year with warm to hot summers and cool winters
tropical	wet and dry seasons, hot all year
continental	wet, warm to hot summers and cold winters

—— country boundary

Arctic Ocean

Arctic Circle

Sea of Okhotsk

Sea of Japan

Black Sea

2

1

IRAQ   IRAN

Red Sea

Arabian Peninsula

Arabian Sea

INDIA

BANGLADESH

Bay of Bengal

SRI LANKA

Tropic of Cancer

Pacific Ocean

N
W   E
S

1. Mediterranean Sea
2. Caspian Sea

Equator

Indian Ocean

The shamal is a dry, dusty summer wind that blows over Iraq, Iran, and the Arabian Peninsula. It blows for about two months—often without stopping. It can cause terrible sandstorms.

It can be very difficult to see when the shamal is blowing.

Southwest and Central Asia's
Plants

Plants in Southwest and Central Asia are well-adapted to the region's many ecosystems, including deserts, forests, and mountains. An ecosystem is all of the living and nonliving things in a certain area. It includes plants, animals, soil, weather ... everything!

Some desert plants use drops of night dew for their water. The plants' leaves trap the water and keep it from evaporating (turning from a liquid to a gas) in the warmth of the day.

Plants that grow in cold places have bunched roots and leaves to hold any warmth and water tightly inside.

Some Plants of Southwest and Central Asia

desert

date palm — The date palm grows well in many parts of Southwest Asia. Its leaves are spiky, and its fruit is small and sticky.

coffee bush — Coffee bush flowers are white and sweet-smelling. They last for a few days, then turn into coffee cherries months later.

forest

pine tree — Pines are a type of evergreen tree. The thick evergreen forests of northern Russia are the largest in the world. They cover an area the size of the United States.

powder puff — The powder puff is a shrub with bright, long-lasting red or pink flowers. It grows well in India's warm, wet climate.

grassland

tulip — Tulips come in every color except blue and true black. Many people believe that the very first tulips came from Asia.

mountain

cedar tree — The cedar tree can be seen on the flag of Lebanon. Cedar trees grow on the low mountains of Lebanon, Syria, and Turkey.

rain forest

Indian lotus — The Indian lotus grows in the rain forest ecosystems of India and the surrounding countries. Lotus flowers may measure up to 8 inches (20 centimeters) across.

tundra

cushion plant — Cushion plants look like flat cushions, or round pillows, on the ground. The leaves are closely packed to protect the plant from wind, ice, and snow.

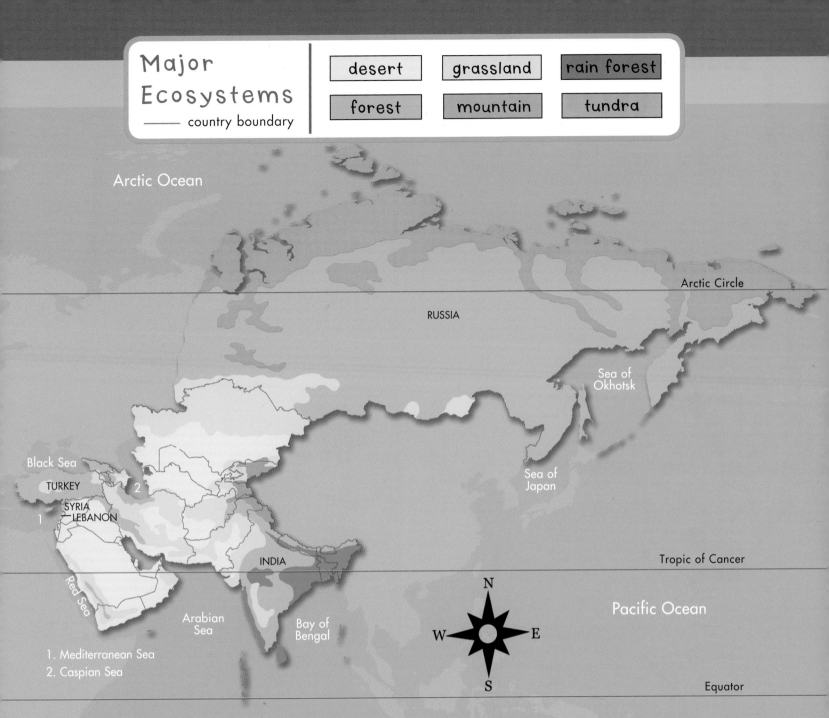

Major Ecosystems

— country boundary

| desert | grassland | rain forest |
| forest | mountain | tundra |

Arctic Ocean

Arctic Circle

RUSSIA

Sea of Okhotsk

Sea of Japan

Black Sea

TURKEY

SYRIA
LEBANON

1

2

Tropic of Cancer

INDIA

Red Sea

Arabian Sea

Bay of Bengal

Pacific Ocean

N

W E

S

1. Mediterranean Sea
2. Caspian Sea

Equator

Indian Ocean

Animals

The animals of Southwest and Central Asia have adapted, or changed, to survive in a wide range of ecosystems. An ecosystem is all of the living and nonliving things in a certain area.

Animals such as the yak and reindeer have shaggy coats to protect them in the cold mountains and tundra. Camels, cobras, and other animals that live in the dry desert can survive on little food and water.

Some Animals of Southwest and Central Asia

desert	Arabian camel	The Arabian (or dromedary) camel has one hump. The hump is filled with fat, not water. The camel uses the fat whenever there is little water or food.	
	cobra	The cobra is a poisonous snake. It lives only in the desert regions of Asia.	
	jerboa	Jerboas have hairs on the bottom of their feet that act as "snowshoes" in the deep desert sand.	
	Arabian oryx	The Arabian oryx is a large antelope that can survive without water for long periods of time.	
tundra	reindeer	The reindeer is a kind of deer that is well-adapted to living in the tundra. It has wide hooves so it can walk easily on soft snow and slippery ice.	

forest	gaur	Gaurs are the largest species of wild cattle in the world. A full-grown male weighs about 1,000 pounds (450 kilograms).
	Siberian tiger	The Siberian tiger is the largest member of the cat family. It lives only in Central Asia.
	Asian elephant	The Asian elephant weighs less than the African elephant, has smaller ears, and has two bumps on its forehead.
	brown bear	Like humans, brown bears are omnivores. They feed on both plants and other animals.
mountain	yak	Yaks have large lungs. They help the animals breathe easier in the thin mountain air.
	lammergeier	The lammergeier is a large, eagle-like bird that lives high in the mountains. It is also called the bearded vulture.

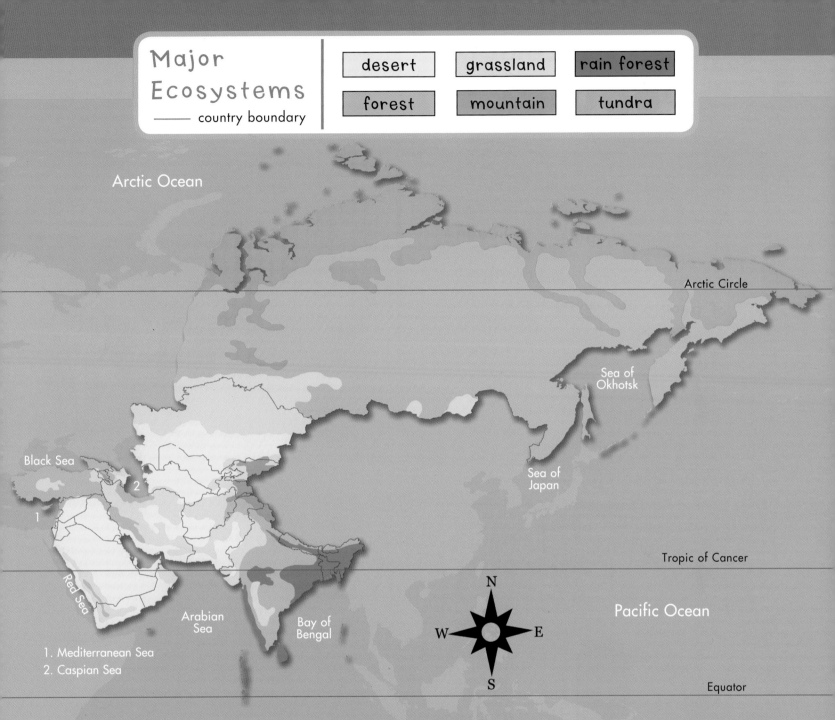

Major Ecosystems

—— country boundary

| desert | grassland | rain forest |
| forest | mountain | tundra |

Arctic Ocean

Arctic Circle

Sea of Okhotsk

Sea of Japan

Black Sea

2

1

Red Sea

Arabian Sea

Bay of Bengal

1. Mediterranean Sea
2. Caspian Sea

Tropic of Cancer

Pacific Ocean

N
W   E
S

Equator

Indian Ocean

Southwest and Central Asia's Population

Much of Southwest and Central Asia is too dry, too mountainous, or too cold for people to live in.

For this reason, huge numbers of people live along the warm coasts and rivers of Pakistan, India, and Bangladesh. These areas average more than 2,000 people per square mile.

Living and working

Dubai, United Arab Emirates, is a fast-growing city. Its native population is so small, however, that 75 percent of the people living and working in Dubai have moved there from other countries around the world.

Tall business buildings rise from the coast of Dubai.

A crowded country

India is home to 1.1 billion people. It is the second-most populated country in the world (only China has more people). And it continues to grow each year. Eight of India's cities have more than 5 million people each.

Passengers crowd onto a train in Mumbai, India.

One big city

Mumbai, once called Bombay, is a busy port city. More than 12 million people live there. It is India's largest (and Southwest and Central Asia's largest) city. Many people come to Mumbai to find work in the textile, technology, and service industries. But with more people than jobs, not everyone can find work.

- Karachi is Pakistan's capital and its largest city. More than 9 million people live there.
- With a population of about 14 million people, Tehran, Iran, is one of the most populated cities in Southwest Asia.
- Yemen is a very young country. Forty-six percent of the population is under 15 years old.

People per Square Mile

- ● place of interest
- —— country boundary

less than 5	5-25	25-125	125-250	more than 250
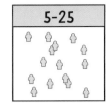	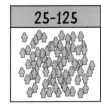		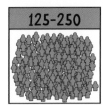	

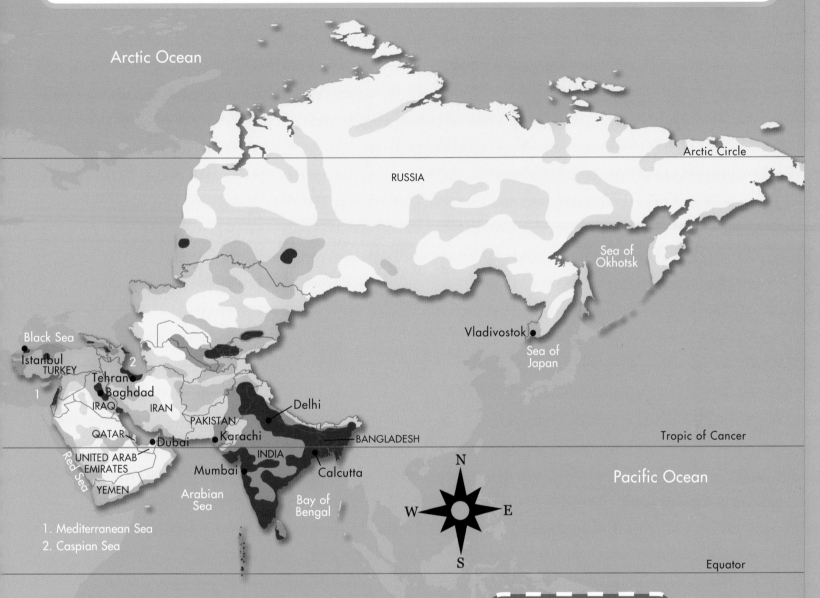

Arctic Ocean

Arctic Circle

RUSSIA

Sea of Okhotsk

Vladivostok

Sea of Japan

Black Sea

Istanbul

TURKEY

2

Tehran

Baghdad

IRAQ

IRAN

1

Delhi

PAKISTAN

QATAR

Karachi

BANGLADESH

Tropic of Cancer

Dubai

INDIA

UNITED ARAB EMIRATES

Red Sea

Mumbai

Calcutta

Pacific Ocean

YEMEN

Arabian Sea

Bay of Bengal

N

W   E

S

1. Mediterranean Sea
2. Caspian Sea

Equator

Indian Ocean

DID YOU KNOW? In parts of Southwest Asia, there are many more men than women. In Qatar, for example, there are almost twice as many men than women.

75

CHAPTER SIX

Far East and Southeast Asia

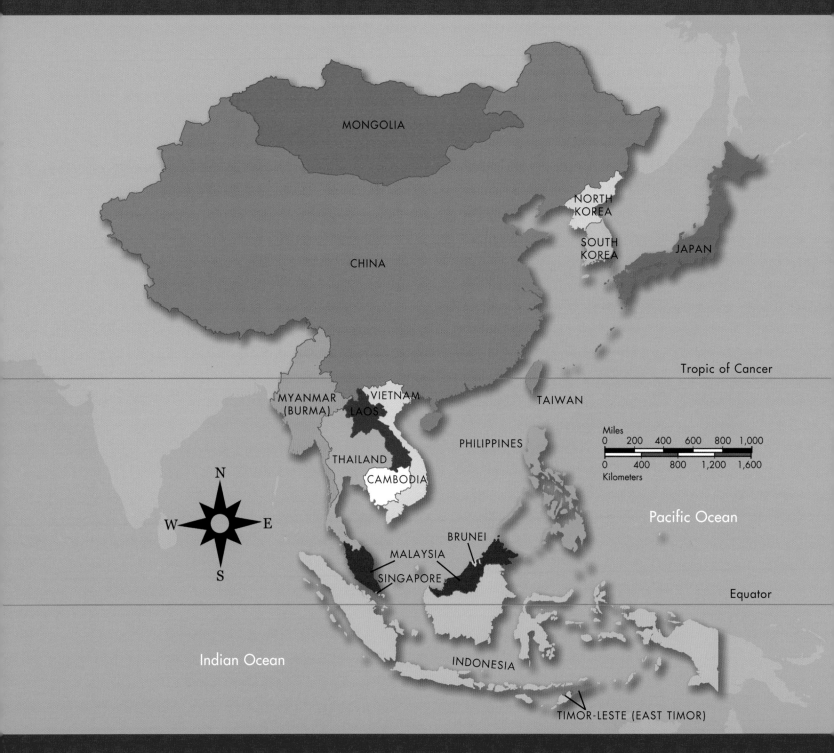

MONGOLIA

NORTH KOREA

SOUTH KOREA

JAPAN

CHINA

Tropic of Cancer

MYANMAR (BURMA)

VIETNAM

LAOS

TAIWAN

THAILAND

PHILIPPINES

Miles
0 200 400 600 800 1,000

0 400 800 1,200 1,600
Kilometers

CAMBODIA

N
W   E
S

BRUNEI

Pacific Ocean

MALAYSIA

SINGAPORE

Equator

Indian Ocean

INDONESIA

TIMOR-LESTE (EAST TIMOR)

BRUNEI

CAMBODIA

CHINA

INDONESIA

JAPAN

LAOS

NORTH KOREA

MALAYSIA

MONGOLIA

MYANMAR
(BURMA)

PHILIPPINES

SINGAPORE

SOUTH KOREA

TAIWAN

THAILAND

TIMOR-LESTE
(EAST TIMOR)

VIETNAM

Continent size: Asia, as a whole, is the largest of Earth's seven continents

Number of countries: 17 in the region, 49 total in Asia

Major languages: Burmese, Chinese Mandarin, English, Filipino, Japanese, Khmer

Total population: 2.1 billion (2009 estimate)

Largest country (land size): China

Most populated country: China

Most populated city: Tokyo, Japan

Climate: mostly dry with hot summers and cold winters in the North; continental (wet, warm to hot summers and cold winters) in the Northeast; cool to cold in the mountains of the West; mild in the East; tropical in the South

Highest point: Mount Everest, Nepal/China, 29,035 feet (8,856 meters)

Lowest point: Turpan Pendi, China, 505 feet (154 m) below sea level

Longest river: Chang Jiang (Yangtze) River

Largest desert: Gobi Desert

Major agricultural products: barley, cassava, coconuts, corn, cotton, jute, palm oil

Major industries: agriculture, fishing, mining, manufacturing (clothing, food and beverage, and electronic equipment)

Natural resources: coal, copper, gold, iron, lead, oil, tin

Far East and Southeast Asia's
Landforms

The Far East and Southeast Asia region is very mountainous.

Smaller mountains cover many of the region's island countries, including Japan, Indonesia, and the Philippines. Some of the world's tallest mountains are in western China.

Across eastern China lie large areas of flat land called plains. Most people in China live on the plains.

Chocolate Hills

The Chocolate Hills are a famous site in the Philippines. There are 1,268 hills, all the same shape and roughly the same size. They are covered with grass that turns chocolate brown at the end of the summer. The color gives the hills their name.

The Chocolate Hills in the Philippines

Ring of Fire

The Ring of Fire is a long chain of volcanoes and earthquake activity that circles much of the Pacific Ocean. More than half of the world's volcanoes lie along the Ring of Fire. A volcano is a type of mountain that throws smoke, ash, and red-hot lava high into the air.

Thousands of volcanic mountains rise out of the ocean along the Ring of Fire.

The world's highest plateau

The huge Tibetan Plateau lies in western China. It is bordered to the north by the Kunlun Mountains and to the south and southwest by the Himalayas. Often called the "Roof of the World," the plateau reaches an average height of 3.1 miles (5 kilometers) above sea level.

- The world's tallest mountains are the Himalayas. They stand along China's southwestern border and include the tallest peak on Earth, Mount Everest. Mount Everest is 29,035 feet (8,856 meters) tall.
- Indonesia is made up of more than 17,500 islands. People live on only 6,000 of them.

Turpan Pendi

Altay Mountains

Mongolian Plateau

Tien Shan Mountains

Gobi Desert

Takla Makan Desert

Kunlun Mountains

North China Plain

Sea of Japan

Korean Peninsula

JAPAN

Mount Fuji

Yellow Sea

Tibetan Plateau

CHINA

Himalayas

East China Sea

Mount Everest

Tropic of Cancer

Bay of Bengal

N
W   E
S

Pacific Ocean

South China Sea

PHILIPPINES

Andaman Sea

Malay Peninsula

Chocolate Hills

Philippine Sea

Celebes Sea

Equator

Indian Ocean

Java Sea

INDONESIA

The largest desert in the Far East and Southeast Asia is the Gobi Desert. Deserts are not landforms, but the Gobi is an important part of the region's landscape. Except for some places in the south, much of the Gobi Desert is covered with rocks and gravel.

Large sand dunes in the southern Gobi Desert

79

The Far East and Southeast Asia are closely tied to many bodies of water.

Long rivers flow across much of the land. Miles and miles of coastline border a number of seas, including the Yellow Sea, the South China Sea, and the Java Sea.

The seas surrounding the Far East and Southeast Asia are part of the Pacific Ocean and the Indian Ocean.

Pirates ahoy!

Pirates still sail the waters of Southeast Asia. But instead of ships, swords, and cannons, today's pirates use speedboats, guns, and cell phones. The South China Sea is one of the busiest trade routes for shipping in the world. It is also the most dangerous. About 150 pirate attacks take place in its waters each year.

Three Gorges Dam

Building the Three Gorges Dam across China's Chang Jiang River was one of the world's largest projects. The dam helps control the flooding of the Chang Jiang, which has taken many lives over the years. It also uses the power of the water to create electricity.

The waters of the Chang Jiang River flow through the Three Gorges Dam.

- The Huang (Yellow) River is China's second-longest river. The river gets its name from the yellow, sandy soil carried along by the water.

- The Mekong River starts in western China and ends in the South China Sea. The land surrounding the river's nine mouths makes up the Mekong Delta.

- The Irrawaddy River flows through the center of Myanmar. It is the country's most important waterway.

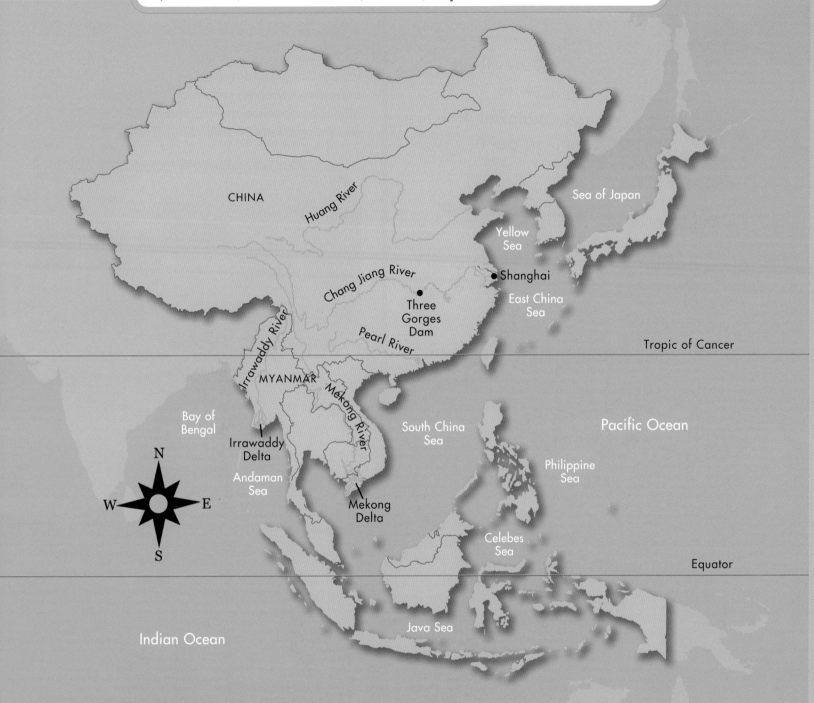

Major Bodies of Water

- place of interest
— country boundary

🔷 lake ⌇ river

CHINA

Huang River

Chang Jiang River

Three
Gorges
Dam

Pearl River

Irrawaddy River

MYANMAR

Mekong River

Sea of Japan

Yellow
Sea

● Shanghai

East China
Sea

Tropic of Cancer

Bay of
Bengal

Irrawaddy
Delta

Andaman
Sea

Mekong
Delta

South China
Sea

Pacific Ocean

Philippine
Sea

Celebes
Sea

Equator

N
W E
S

Java Sea

Indian Ocean

The Chang Jiang River (also called the Yangtze) is the longest
river in China and the third-longest river in the world. It flows
through steep valleys toward the sea. Its wide mouth lies near
the city of Shanghai.

The Chang Jiang River is busy with boat traffic.

81

Climate is the average weather a place has from season to season, year to year. Rainfall and temperature play large parts in a region's climate.

While most of the countries near the equator and the Tropic of Cancer have a tropical climate, countries farther north have a wider range.

China is such a huge country that five different types of climates can be found there: dry, continental, mountain, mild, and tropical.

El Niño

El Niño is the nickname for a strange weather pattern that hits many southern parts of the world every two to seven years. Scientists believe it is caused by an unusual warming of the Pacific Ocean off the coast of Indonesia. During El Niño years, storms, droughts (times of no rain), and floods are common.

Monsoon seasons

The monsoons are strong winds that blow off the Indian Ocean and the South China Sea. These winds bring two seasons, known as the monsoon seasons. Monsoon seasons are marked by heavy rainfall and tropical windstorms called hurricanes.

Gusty winds blow during the monsoon seasons.

Climate basics

A region's climate depends upon three major things: how close it is to the ocean, how high up it is, and how close it is to the equator. Areas along the ocean have milder climates than areas farther inland. The higher a region is, and the farther it is from the equator, the colder its temperature.

- Indonesia receives an average of 7 to 11 inches (18 to 28 centimeters) of rain each month. The heaviest amounts fall during the wet season—November to April.
- Winter in Mongolia is long and cold. The average winter temperature is minus 4 degrees Fahrenheit (minus 20 degrees Celsius). Some nights can dip down to minus 40 F (minus 40 C).

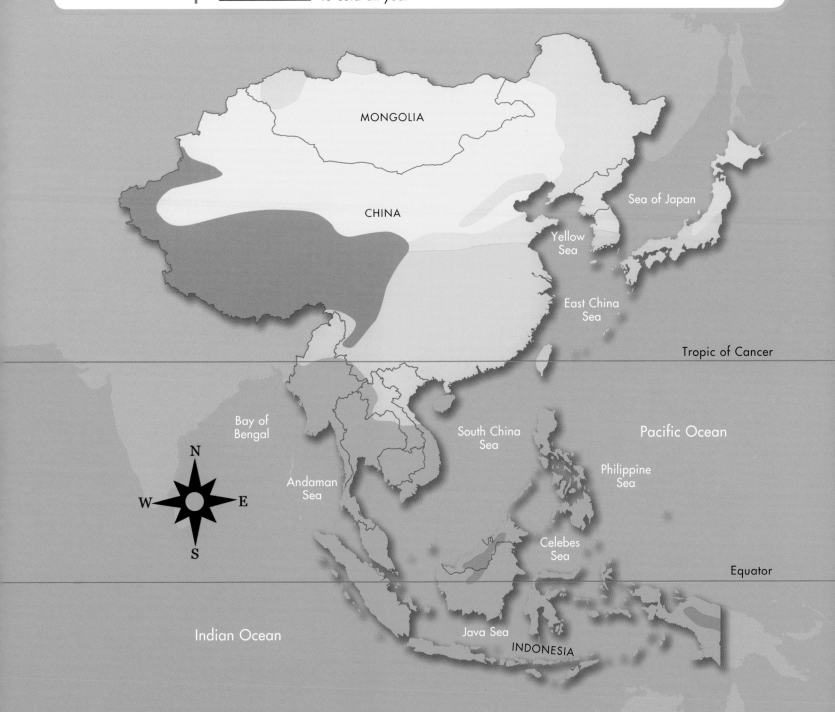

Climate

_____ country boundary

dry — dry most or all year with hot summers and warm to cold winters

tropical — wet and dry seasons, hot all year

mountain — wet and dry seasons, cool to cold all year

mild — wet winters or all year with warm to hot summers and cool winters

continental — wet, warm to hot summers and cold winters

MONGOLIA

CHINA

Sea of Japan

Yellow Sea

East China Sea

Tropic of Cancer

Bay of Bengal

N
W E
S

Andaman Sea

South China Sea

Pacific Ocean

Philippine Sea

Celebes Sea

Equator

Indian Ocean

Java Sea

INDONESIA

Far East and Southeast Asia's
Plants

Plants in the Far East and Southeast Asia are well-adapted to the region's many ecosystems, including deserts, grasslands, rain forests, and mountains. An ecosystem is all of the living and nonliving things in a certain area. It includes plants, animals, soil, weather ... everything!

The rain forests of Southeast Asia are like large, layered greenhouses. The top layers get a lot of sunlight, while the layers along the forest floor get very little. Some plants, such as vines, adapt to these conditions by climbing trees to reach the sunlight.

Some Plants of the Far East and Southeast Asia

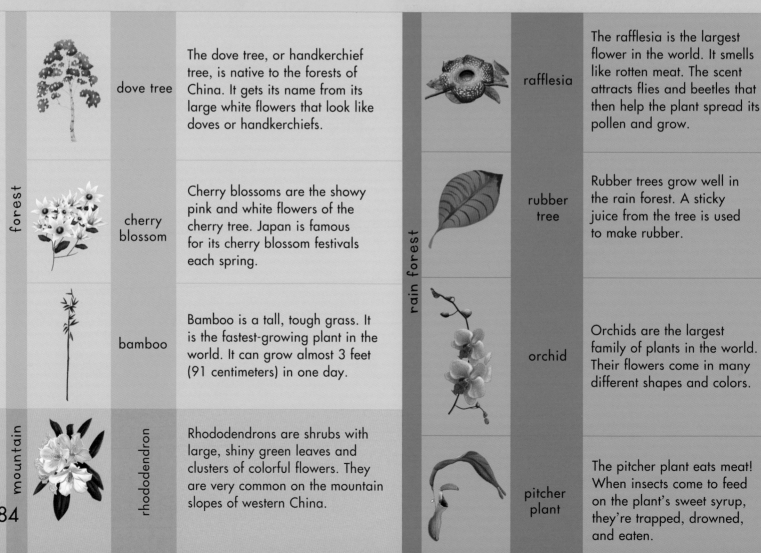

forest

dove tree — The dove tree, or handkerchief tree, is native to the forests of China. It gets its name from its large white flowers that look like doves or handkerchiefs.

cherry blossom — Cherry blossoms are the showy pink and white flowers of the cherry tree. Japan is famous for its cherry blossom festivals each spring.

bamboo — Bamboo is a tall, tough grass. It is the fastest-growing plant in the world. It can grow almost 3 feet (91 centimeters) in one day.

mountain

rhododendron — Rhododendrons are shrubs with large, shiny green leaves and clusters of colorful flowers. They are very common on the mountain slopes of western China.

rain forest

rafflesia — The rafflesia is the largest flower in the world. It smells like rotten meat. The scent attracts flies and beetles that then help the plant spread its pollen and grow.

rubber tree — Rubber trees grow well in the rain forest. A sticky juice from the tree is used to make rubber.

orchid — Orchids are the largest family of plants in the world. Their flowers come in many different shapes and colors.

pitcher plant — The pitcher plant eats meat! When insects come to feed on the plant's sweet syrup, they're trapped, drowned, and eaten.

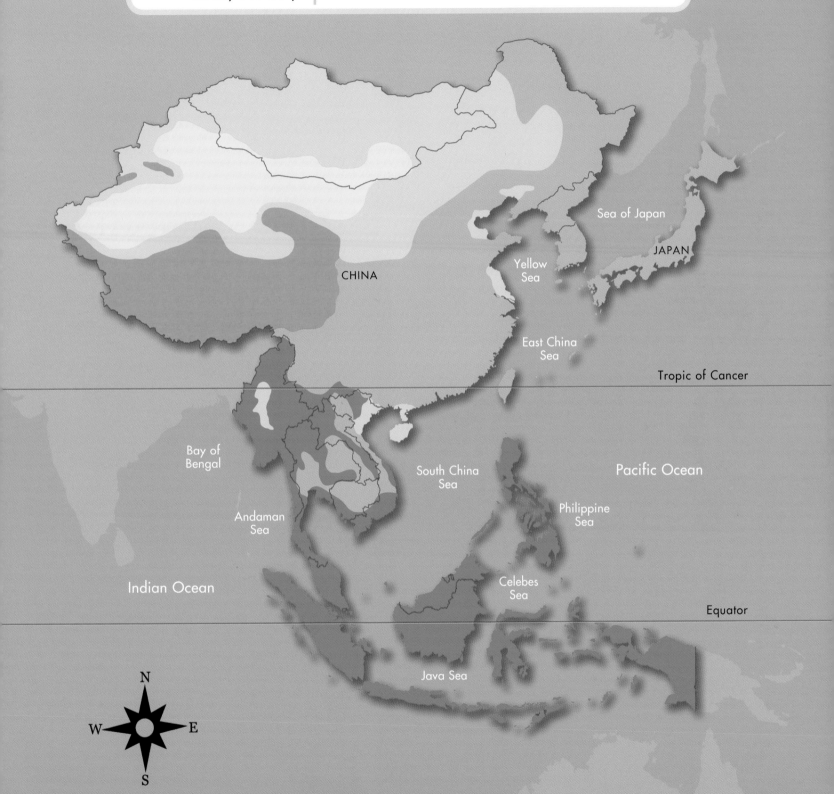

Major Ecosystems

country boundary

desert   grassland   rain forest
forest   mountain

CHINA

JAPAN

Sea of Japan

Yellow Sea

East China Sea

Tropic of Cancer

Bay of Bengal

Andaman Sea

South China Sea

Pacific Ocean

Philippine Sea

Celebes Sea

Indian Ocean

Equator

Java Sea

N
W   E
S

Far East and Southeast Asia's
Animals

Many different kinds of animals live in the Far East and Southeast Asia. All are well-adapted to the ecosystems in which they live. An ecosystem is all of the living and nonliving things in a certain area.

Animals of the Far East and Southeast Asia include mammals such as camels, elephants, and leopards; birds such as cranes, ducks, and parrots; reptiles such as snakes and turtles; many kinds of fish; and thousands of insect species.

Some Animals of the Far East and Southeast Asia

desert	Bactrian camel	The Bactrian camel has two humps. The humps are filled with fat, not water. The camel uses the fat whenever there is little water or food.
forest	giant panda	Wild giant pandas are found only in a few forests in central China. Bamboo makes up 99 percent of their diet.
	Asian elephant	The Asian elephant weighs less than the African elephant, has smaller ears, and has two bumps on its forehead.
	flying lizard	The flying lizard can extend its limbs to make "wings" and glide between trees.
	water buffalo	People use water buffalo for meat, milk, and the plowing work they do.
	red-crowned crane	One of the largest breeding areas for red-crowned cranes is northern Japan.

rain forest	Sumatran rhinoceros	Sumatran rhinoceroses are the smallest and rarest rhinos in the world. Most of them live on the island of Sumatra.
	orangutan	Orangutans spend most of their lives in trees. They use their long arms to swing from branch to branch.
grassland	Komodo dragon	The Komodo dragon is the largest lizard in the world. It lives only on small patches of grassland on a few Indonesian islands.
mountain	snow leopard	The snow leopard's fur is long and woolly. It helps protect the cat in cold weather.
	Pallas' cat	The Pallas' cat is about the size of a housecat. It feeds mostly on small, rabbit-like animals called pikas.
	Tibetan yak	Tibetan yaks have large lungs. They help the animals breathe easier in the thin mountain air.

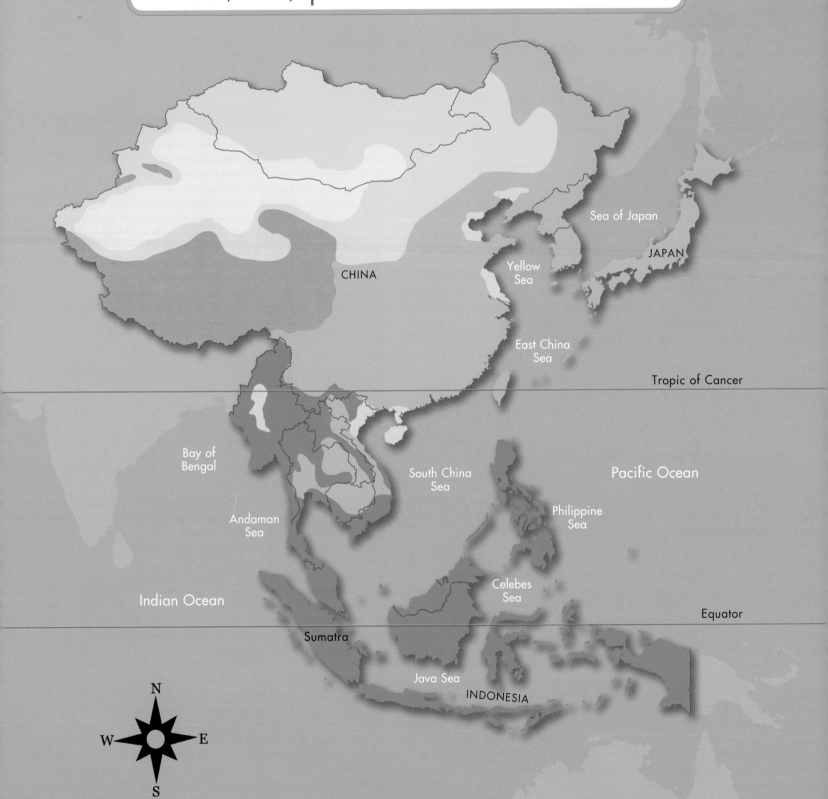

Major Ecosystems

— country boundary

| desert | grassland | rain forest |
| forest | mountain | |

CHINA

Sea of Japan

JAPAN

Yellow
Sea

East China
Sea

Tropic of Cancer

Bay of
Bengal

South China
Sea

Pacific Ocean

Andaman
Sea

Philippine
Sea

Celebes
Sea

Indian Ocean

Equator

Sumatra

Java Sea

INDONESIA

N
W   E
S

Far East and Southeast Asia's
Population

Large numbers of people in the Far East and Southeast Asia live near the coasts. The oceans are a source of jobs, food, and fun.

Large numbers of people also live on the plains of China. The land and climate there are perfect for growing crops.

China has 20 percent of the world's population. The Far East and Southeast Asia is where the world's population is growing fastest. By the year 2050, 60 percent of all of the people on Earth will be living in Asia.

People!

More people live in China than in any other country in the world. About 1.3 billion people live there. More than one-fourth of them are younger than 14 years old. The capital city is Beijing. The city and the surrounding area is home to nearly 11 million people.

A Chinese girl

Four big cities

Tokyo is the capital of Japan. With 35 million people in the city and surrounding area, Tokyo is the most-populated city in the world. It is a center of international business.

The streets of Tokyo are very crowded.

Nearly 10 million people live in **Seoul**, the capital of South Korea. That number is about one-fourth of South Korea's total population.

Shanghai is the most-populated city in China. Almost 13 million people live there. Once a sleepy fishing town, Shanghai has become China's fastest-growing city. Some of the tallest buildings in the world are found in Shanghai.

Jakarta, Indonesia, is home to more than 12 million people. It is the country's capital, largest port city, and center of transportation and industry.

- In Myanmar, two-thirds of the population live along the Irrawaddy River.
- Mongolia is fairly large—it's twice the size of the U.S. state of Texas—but it has fewer people per square mile than any other country in the world.
- Indonesia is the fourth-most populated country in the world. Only China, India, and the United States have more people.

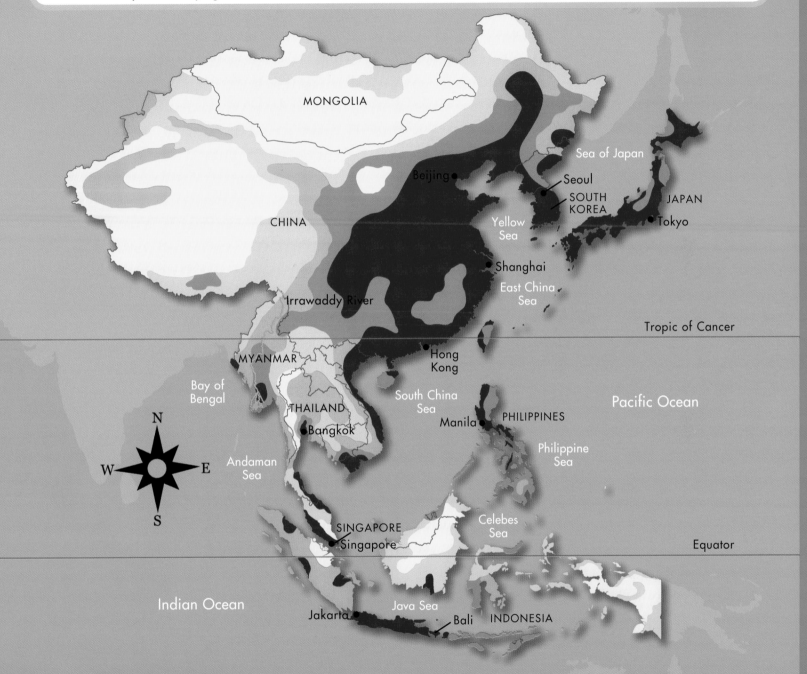

People per Square Mile

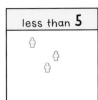 less than **5**

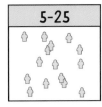 **5-25**

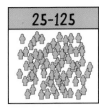 **25-125**

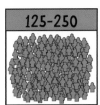 **125-250**

 more than **250**

● place of interest

——— country boundary

MONGOLIA

CHINA

Beijing ●

Irrawaddy River

Yellow Sea

Sea of Japan

Seoul ●
SOUTH KOREA

JAPAN

Tokyo ●

Shanghai ●

East China Sea

Tropic of Cancer

MYANMAR

Hong Kong ●

Bay of Bengal

THAILAND

Bangkok ●

South China Sea

Manila ●

PHILIPPINES

Philippine Sea

Pacific Ocean

Andaman Sea

N
W · E
S

Celebes Sea

SINGAPORE
Singapore ●

Indian Ocean

Java Sea

Jakarta ●

Bali

INDONESIA

Equator

The beautiful islands of Southeast Asia attract many tourists. These visitors can double the size of the islands' population. The island of Bali, Indonesia, is home to 3 million people. But it welcomes another 3 million people as tourists each year.

People in Bali, Indonesia, enjoy warm weather, sandy beaches, and colorful sunsets.

89

CHAPTER SEVEN

Australia

Equator

Indian Ocean

Tropic of Capricorn

AUSTRALIA

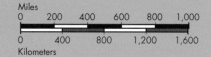

Miles
0   200   400   600   800   1,000

0   400   800   1,200   1,600
Kilometers

Pacific Ocean

NEW ZEALAND

N
W   E
S

AUSTRALIA   NEW ZEALAND

Continent size: the smallest of Earth's seven continents

Number of countries: one

Major languages: Aboriginal languages, Chinese, English, Italian

Total population: 21.2 million (2009 estimate)

Most populated city: Sydney

Climate: dry most or all year with hot summers and warm to cold winters throughout most of the continent; tropical in the far north and northeast; mild in the far southwest, southeast, and eastern coast

Highest point: Mount Kosciuszko, 7,356 feet (2,229 meters)

Lowest point: Lake Eyre, 50 feet (15 m) below sea level

Longest river: Murray River

Largest body of water: Lake Eyre

Largest desert: Great Victoria Desert

Major agricultural products: barley, cattle, dairy products, fruits, poultry, sheep, sugarcane, wheat

Major industries: agriculture, fishing, manufacturing (transportation equipment, chemicals, and steel), mining

Natural resources: bauxite, coal, copper, diamonds, gold, iron ore, lead, mineral sands, natural gas, nickel, petroleum, silver, tungsten, uranium, zinc

Oceania

Australia is the only continent that is also a country. Australia is part of a region called Oceania, which is made up of more than 25,000 islands in the Pacific Ocean. New Zealand is one of the largest countries of Oceania. It is divided into two islands—the North Island and the South Island. New Zealand's capital is Wellington, which is on the North Island.

Australia's Landforms

Australia can be divided into three sections—the Western Plateau, the Central Lowlands, and the Eastern Highlands.

The Western Plateau covers more than 65 percent of the continent's total area. It contains a number of large deserts.

The Central Lowlands stretch across several basins.

The continent's largest mountain range is the Great Dividing Mountain Range, which is also known as the Eastern Highlands. These mountains stretch across the east coast of Australia and divide the east coast from the rest of the country.

The Cape York Peninsula

The Cape York Peninsula in northeastern Australia is truly wild. Almost the entire 54,000 square miles (140,400 square kilometers) of the peninsula is wilderness. There are only about 18,000 people who live on the Cape York Peninsula, and more than half of them are Aborigine people.

Uluru

Also known as Ayers Rock, Uluru is a giant sandstone rock that rises out of the middle of the continent. It is 1,142 feet (348 meters) high and about 6 miles (9.6 kilometers) around its base. Uluru is one of the largest single rock formations on Earth. The native Aborigine people consider Uluru to be a holy place.

Uluru glows red during sunrises and sunsets.

The Outback

The Outback makes up more than 70 percent of Australia's interior. Its landscape contains many deserts, including the Great Sandy Desert, the Gibson Desert, and the Great Victoria Desert. Deserts are not landforms, but they make up an important part of the continent's landscape. The Outback also contains the MacDonnel Mountains and Hamersley Mountains.

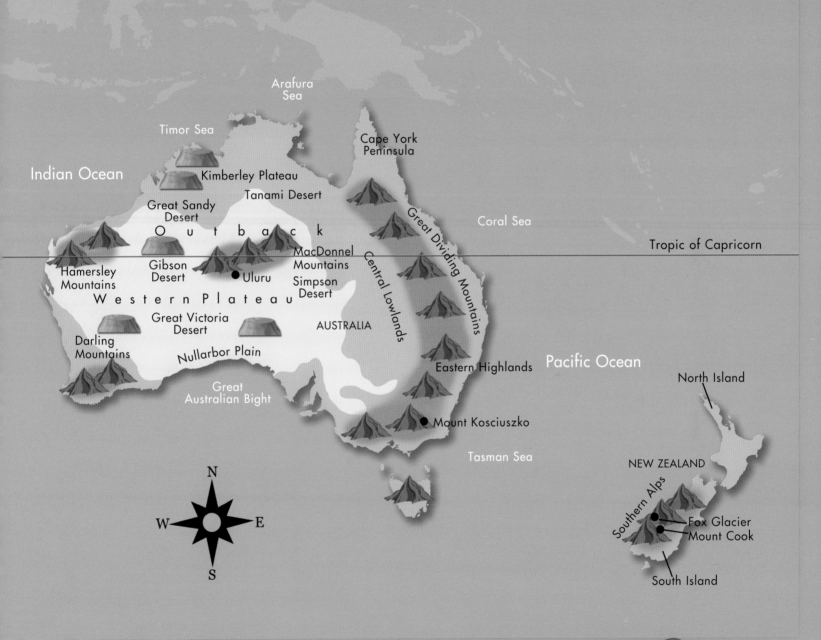

Equator

Arafura Sea

Timor Sea

Indian Ocean

Cape York Peninsula

Kimberley Plateau

Tanami Desert

Coral Sea

Great Sandy Desert

O u t b a c k

Tropic of Capricorn

Hamersley Mountains

Gibson Desert

MacDonnel Mountains

● Uluru

W e s t e r n   P l a t e a u

Simpson Desert

Central Lowlands

Great Victoria Desert

AUSTRALIA

Pacific Ocean

Darling Mountains

Nullarbor Plain

Eastern Highlands

North Island

Great Australian Bight

● Mount Kosciuszko

Tasman Sea

NEW ZEALAND

Southern Alps

● Fox Glacier
● Mount Cook

South Island

N

W   E

S

The Southern Alps stretch across the South Island of New Zealand. Mount Cook, at a height of 12,316 feet (3,756 m), is the country's highest mountain.

The Southern Alps

- The southwestern part of New Zealand's North Island has several active volcanoes. In this area, there are also many hot springs.
- Fox Glacier, on New Zealand's South Island, is less than 982 feet (300 meters) above sea level.

93

Australia's
Bodies of Water

Australia is surrounded by bodies of water. The Indian Ocean lies to the west, and the Pacific Ocean lies to the east. Many seas also border the continent. These include the Timor, the Arafura, the Coral, and the Tasman.

Some of Australia's rivers and lakes, such as Lake Eyre, are mostly dry during parts of the year. Lake Eyre is the largest lake on the continent. It is a salt lake and has completely filled with water only three times during the last 100 years.

Great Australian Bight

The Great Australian Bight is a large, open bay off the southern coast of Australia. Because it receives very little runoff from the deserts that lie to the north, the Great Australian Bight does not have much life in its waters. However, sharks and whales are known to show up there.

The longest river

The Murray River is Australia's longest river. It stretches through more than 1,562 miles (2,520 kilometers) of land. During the 1800s, steamboats carried goods from one end of the river to the other. When the railroads were built, river traffic slowed. Today, people travel the Murray River mostly for fun.

The Murray River

Lake Taupo

Lake Taupo is located on New Zealand's North Island. It is the largest freshwater lake in the country. Underneath its still, blue waters lies the world's most destructive volcano. But it hasn't erupted in the past 26,000 years. A volcano is a kind of mountain that can throw hot, melted rock (lava), ashes, and gases from deep inside the earth.

Lake Taupo

Major Bodies of Water

● place of interest

lake   river

Equator

Arafura Sea

Timor Sea

Daly River

Indian Ocean

Victoria River

Fitzroy River

Coral Sea

Tropic of Capricorn

AUSTRALIA

Lake Eyre

Cooper's Creek

Barwon River

Darling River

Lachlan River

Pacific Ocean

Great Australian Bight

Murray River

● Snowy Mountains

North Island

Waikato River

Lake Taupo

Wanganui River

NEW ZEALAND

Bass Strait

Tasman Sea

Cook Strait

Lake Te Anau

Waitaki River

Clutha River

N
W   E
S

Australia's Climate

Climate is the average weather a place has from season to season, year to year. Rainfall and temperature play large parts in a region's climate.

Australia lies just south of the equator, so its climate is warm.

It is also very dry. In fact, Australia is the second-driest continent on Earth.

Seasons

Because Australia and New Zealand lie beneath the equator, the seasons there are opposite of those in areas such as the United States and Europe, which lie above the equator.

Summer: December to February
Fall: March to May
Winter: June to August
Spring: September to November

Tropical North

Northern Australia is tropical, with hot temperatures and a lot of humidity. Here, there are wet and dry seasons. The hotter wet season usually lasts from December to March. The cooler dry season is usually from May to October.

During the wet season, the tropical north region has still pools of water called billabongs.

Climate basics

A region's climate depends upon three major things: how close it is to the ocean, how high up it is, and how close it is to the equator. Areas along the ocean have milder climates than areas farther inland. The higher a region is, and the farther it is from the equator, the colder its temperature.

- The northeastern coast of Australia is the wettest part of the continent.
- In Australia, snow falls high in the Australian Alps and in some of the mountains of Tasmania.

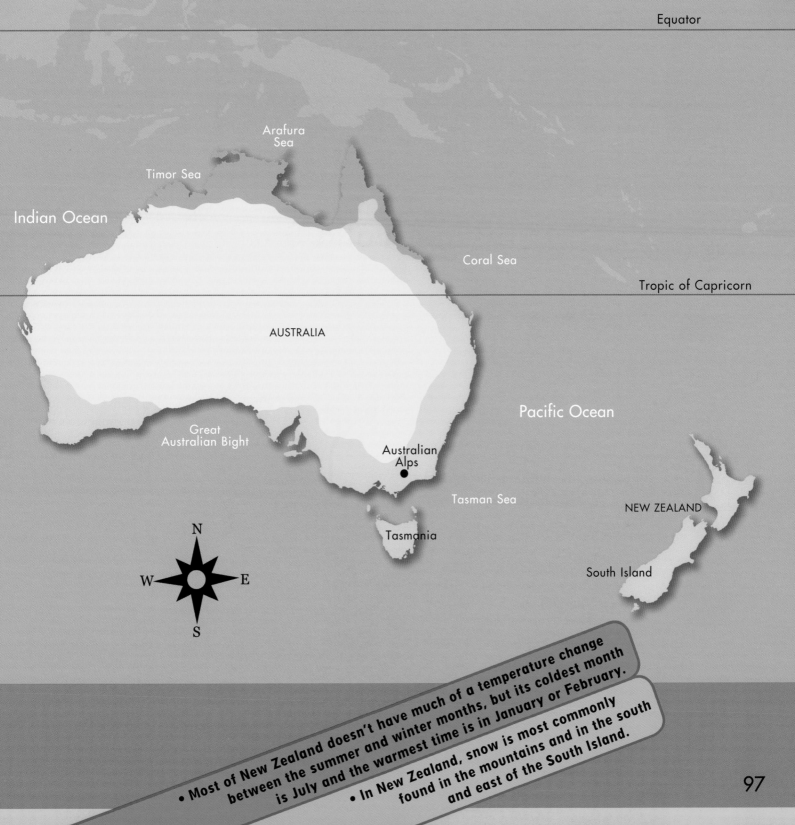

Climate

● place of interest

dry	dry most or all year with hot summers and warm to cold winters
tropical	wet and dry seasons, hot all year
mild	wet winters or all year with warm to hot summers and cool winters

Equator

Arafura Sea

Timor Sea

Indian Ocean

Coral Sea

Tropic of Capricorn

AUSTRALIA

Pacific Ocean

Great Australian Bight

Australian Alps

NEW ZEALAND

Tasman Sea

Tasmania

South Island

N
W   E
S

- Most of New Zealand doesn't have much of a temperature change between the summer and winter months, but its coldest month is July and the warmest time is in January or February.
- In New Zealand, snow is most commonly found in the mountains and in the south and east of the South Island.

Australia's Plants

Because Australia is so far from other lands, many of its plants are found nowhere else in the world. They are well-adapted to the continent's ecosystems. An ecosystem is all of the living and nonliving things in a certain area. It includes plants, animals, soil, weather … everything!

In the wet rain forests that are along Australia's northeastern coast, trees grow tall and close together. Farther inland, there is less rainfall and the trees are shorter and are spread apart amid grasses and shrubs. Tough-leaved bushes are found throughout Australia's interior.

Some Plants of Australia and New Zealand

desert		saltbush	The saltbush grows in dry areas and does well in salty soil.		
		boab tree	Boab trees are found only in northwestern Australia. They have very large trunks in which they store water.		
		spinifex	Spinifex is a spiky grass that covers about 20 percent of Australia. It is found in sandy soil and grows in a short dome shape.		
forest		eucalyptus tree	Different kinds of eucalyptus trees, or gum trees, grow all over Australia. Their leaves produce an oil that can be toxic.		

forest		golden wattle	The golden wattle is Australia's national flower. It is found mostly in southeastern Australia and has long green leaves and small yellow flowers.
		kangaroo paw	The flowering plant called kangaroo paw looks like a kangaroo's hind foot. It grows naturally only in Australia's southwestern forests.
grassland		orchid	There are hundreds of different kinds of orchids in Australia. One kind grows underground and never sees sunlight. Orchids always have a large upper petal.
mountain		kauri tree	The kauri tree is found only on New Zealand's North Island. Its bark is flaky, and its leaves are leathery. It can reach a height of 165 feet (50 meters).
rain forest		mangrove tree	The mangrove tree has long roots that hold the trunk of the tree above water. The roots develop small holes through which the tree can take in air.

98

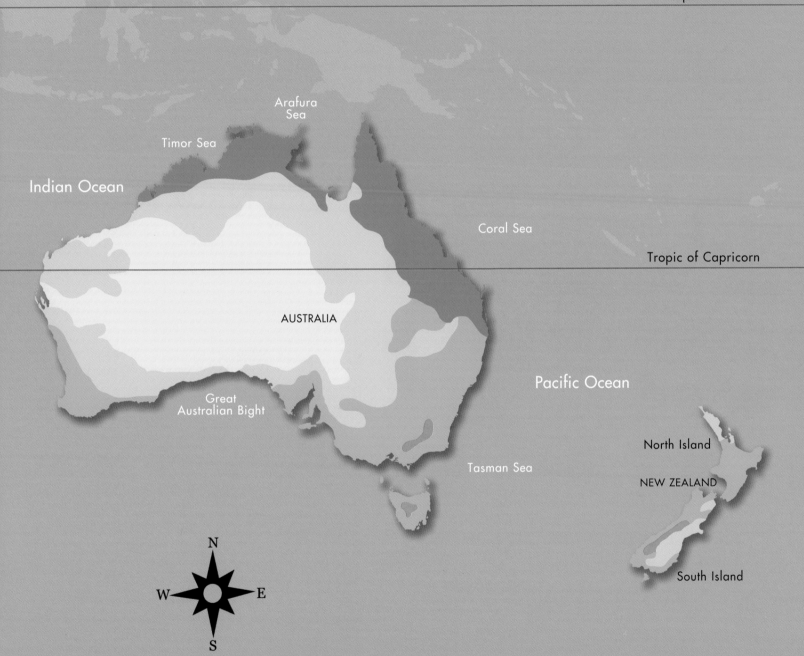

Major Ecosystems

desert   grassland   rain forest

forest   mountain

Equator

Arafura Sea

Timor Sea

Indian Ocean

Coral Sea

Tropic of Capricorn

AUSTRALIA

Pacific Ocean

Great Australian Bight

Tasman Sea

North Island

NEW ZEALAND

South Island

N
W   E
S

Australia's Animals

Because Australia is far from the other continents, many of its animals aren't found anywhere else in the world. A number of them are well-adapted to the desert ecosystem. An ecosystem is all of the living and nonliving things in a certain area.

Just off the northeastern coast of Australia lies the Great Barrier Reef. It is the world's largest coral reef. The reef is made up of skeletons that are produced by millions of small animals called coral polyps.

Some Animals of Australia and New Zealand

desert	king brown snake	The king brown snake is one of the largest snakes in Australia. It is also one of the most poisonous. It can grow to be 10 feet (3.3 meters) long.
	desert death adder	The desert death adder is one of the most poisonous snakes in the world. The snake uses its tail to attract prey.
	dingo	The dingo is a wild dog found in the Outback. A dingo eats kangaroos and other animals.
	kangaroo	A kangaroo is a marsupial. It carries its baby in a pouch, a pocket of skin on its belly.
	wombat	The wombat escapes the hot desert sun by burrowing deep underground.

forest	laughing kookaburra	The laughing kookaburra has a large head and long beak. It is famous for its call, which sounds like a human laugh.
	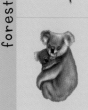 koala	Koalas are marsupials. They feed on eucalyptus leaves and sleep about 20 hours a day.
grassland	redback spider	The redback spider is common throughout Australia. The female has a yellow or red marking on its back. Its bite is poisonous.
mountain	emu	The emu is a bird that can't fly. The emu's long, powerful legs allow it to run as fast as 30 miles (50 kilometers) per hour.
rain forest	 frilled lizard	When the frilled lizard is scared, it opens its mouth and shows a collar of skin around its neck.
	duck-billed platypus	The duck-billed platypus spends most of its time in ponds and streams. The platypus uses its bill to take in water and food such as shrimp, snails, and worms.

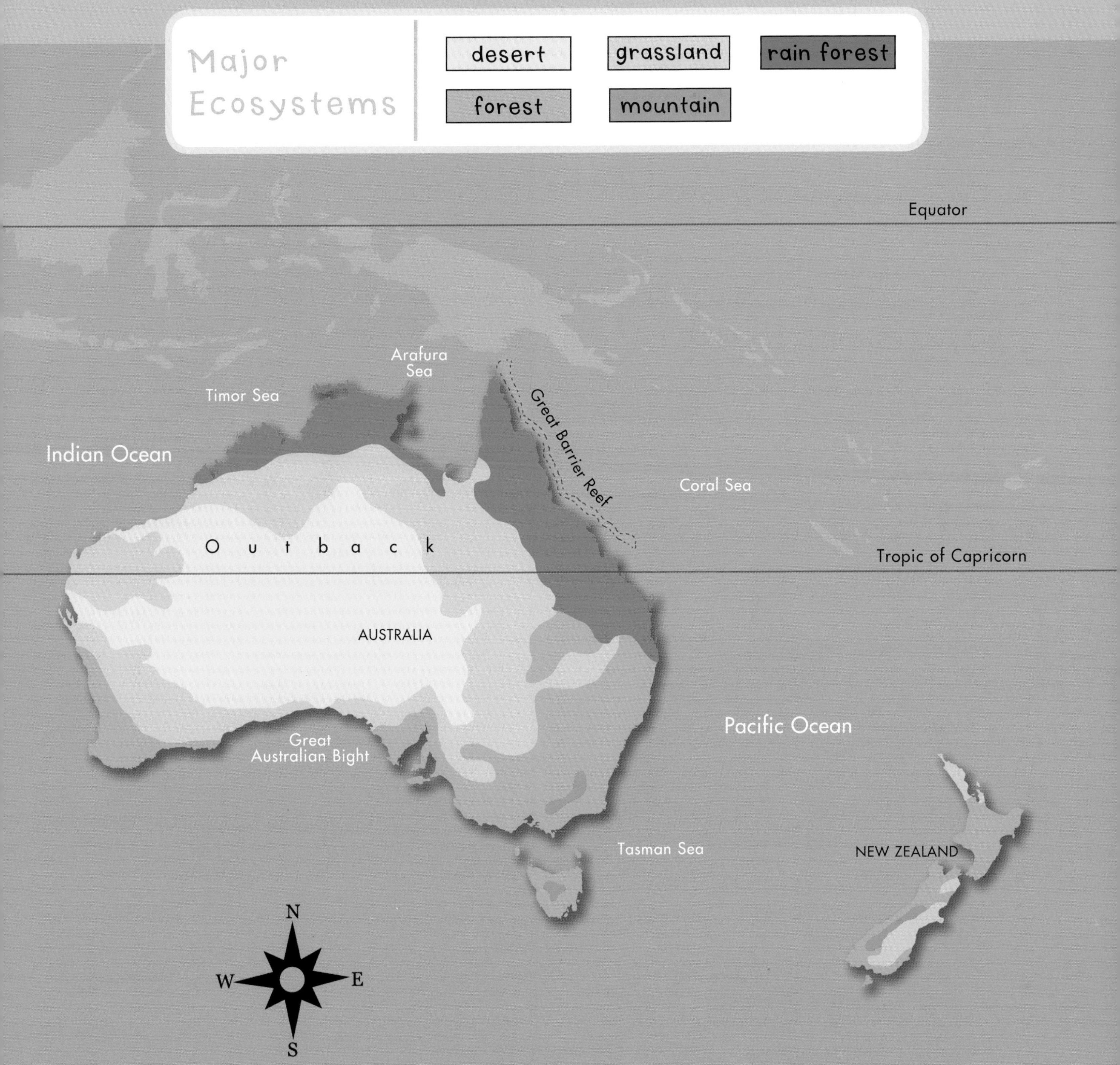

Major Ecosystems

desert	grassland	rain forest
forest	mountain	

Equator

Arafura
Sea

Timor Sea

Indian Ocean

Great Barrier Reef

Coral Sea

O u t b a c k

Tropic of Capricorn

AUSTRALIA

Pacific Ocean

Great
Australian Bight

Tasman Sea

NEW ZEALAND

N
W   E
S

Australia's Population

Australia's population is slightly more than 21 million. Many people live in the big coastal cities, such as Sydney, Melbourne, and Brisbane, because of the mild climate in those areas.

Most Australians have come from Europe. Many of them moved to Australia during the past 200 years. They enjoy the warm climate, the outdoor lifestyle, and new job opportunities. Native Aborigines make up about 1 percent of the total population.

Native people

Australia's Northern Territory is home to the largest Aboriginal population in the country. In fact, Aborigines make up about 25 percent of the Northern Territory's population. The largest Aboriginal reserve in the Northern Territory is called Arnhem Land. About 16,000 Aborigines live there.

Aborigine children

Four big cities

With about 4.4 million residents, **Sydney** is Australia's most populated city. Located on the southeastern coast, it is home to many popular beaches and famous landmarks, such as the Sydney Opera House and the Harbour Bridge.

The Sydney Opera House and Harbour Bridge

With about 4 million people, Australia's second-most populated city is **Melbourne**. It is home to many of Australia's largest companies, such as National Australia Bank.

Brisbane, located on the east coast of Australia, is the country's third-most populated city. It has about 2 million residents.

Perth is Australia's fourth-most populated city, with 1.6 million people. It is the largest city located on the west coast. Perth has the fastest-growing population of all of the major cities in Australia.

People per Square Mile

● place of interest

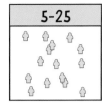 less than **5**

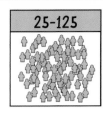 **5-25**

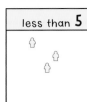 **25-125**

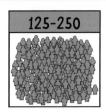 **125-250**

 more than **250**

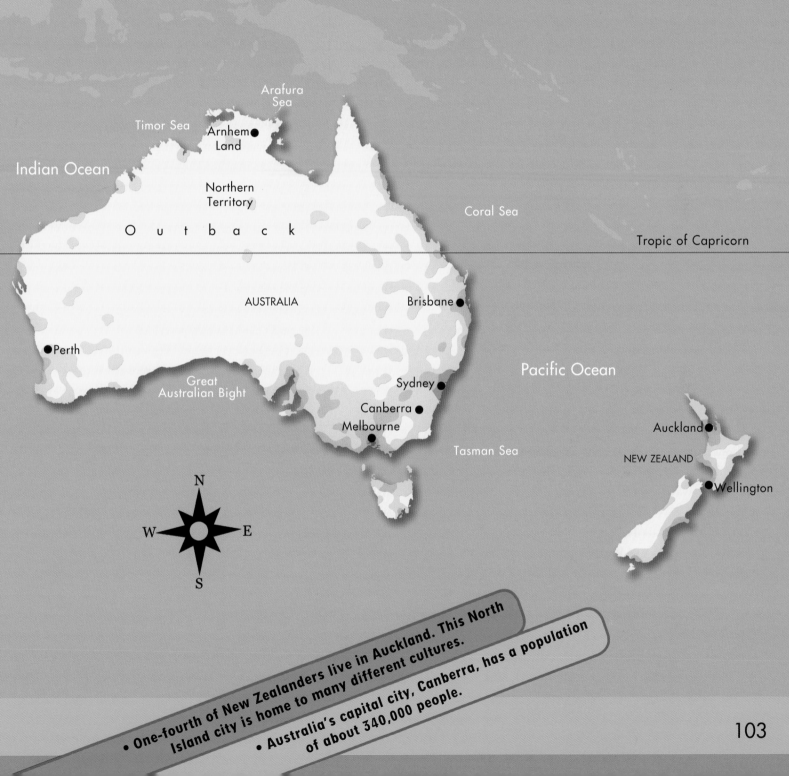

Equator

Arafura Sea

Timor Sea

Arnhem Land ●

Indian Ocean

Northern Territory

Coral Sea

O u t b a c k

Tropic of Capricorn

AUSTRALIA

Brisbane ●

● Perth

Great Australian Bight

Pacific Ocean

Sydney ●

Canberra ●

Auckland ●

Melbourne ●

NEW ZEALAND

Tasman Sea

● Wellington

N
W ✦ E
S

- One-fourth of New Zealanders live in Auckland. This North Island city is home to many different cultures.

- Australia's capital city, Canberra, has a population of about 340,000 people.

103

CHAPTER EIGHT

Poles and Oceans

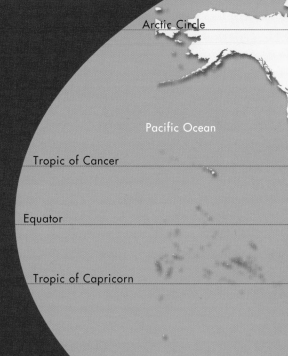

Antarctica

Size: 5.4 million square miles
(14 million square kilometers)

Population: no native inhabitants;
research stations are staffed by about
1,000 people in the winter and about
4,400 people in the summer

Average temperature:
summer: 20 degrees Fahrenheit
(minus 6.7 degrees Celsius)
winter: minus 30 degrees Fahrenheit
(minus 34.4 degrees Celsius)

Highest point: Vinson Massif, 16,067 feet
(4,900 meters)

Lowest point: Bentley Subglacial Trench,
8,432 feet (2,555 m) below sea level

Common animals: elephant seal,
emperor penguin, icefish, petrel

First person to reach the South Pole:
Roald Amundsen, 1912

The Arctic

Size: 8 million square miles
(21 million square km)

Population: about 4 million

Average temperature:
summer: 32 degrees
Fahrenheit
(0 degrees Celsius)
winter: 15 degrees Fahrenheit
(minus 9.4 degrees Celsius)

Highest point: Gunnbjornsfjeld, 12,136 feet
(3,701 m)

Lowest point: Fram Basin, 15,395 feet (4,695 m)
below sea level

Common animals: arctic hare, brown bear, ermine,
musk ox, polar bear, reindeer

First person to reach the North Pole:
Robert Edwin Peary, 1909

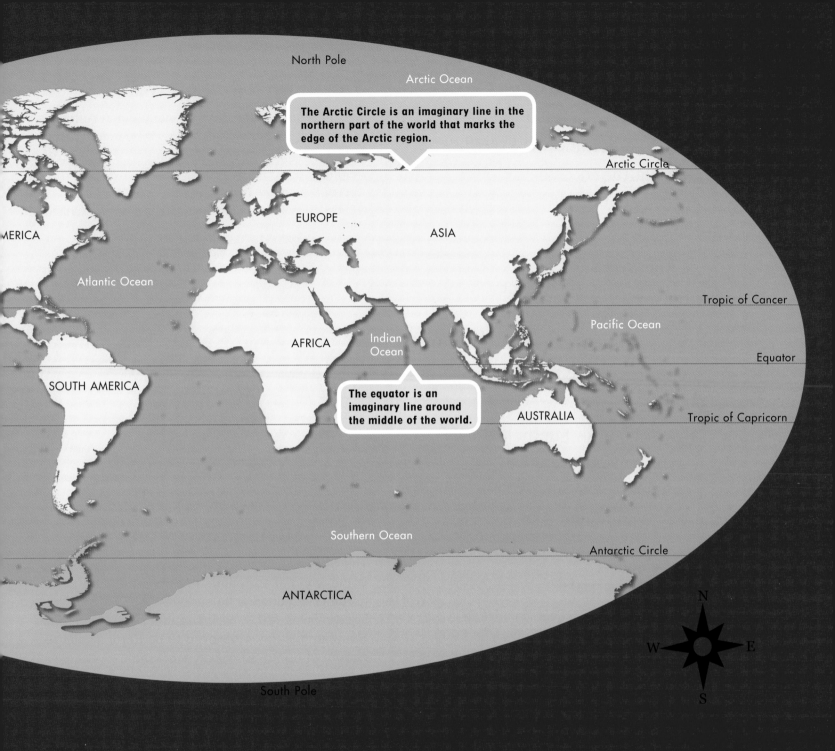

Oceans

Number of oceans: 5—the Pacific Ocean, the Atlantic Ocean, the Indian Ocean, the Arctic Ocean, and the Southern Ocean

Largest ocean (surface area): Pacific Ocean

Smallest ocean (surface area): Arctic Ocean

Deepest ocean (average depth): Pacific Ocean

Deepest point: Mariana Trench, Pacific Ocean, nearly 7 miles (11 km) from water's surface to the ocean floor

Antarctica

Antarctica is the fifth-largest of Earth's seven continents. It lies in the most southern region of the world. It is surrounded by the Southern Ocean.

Except for a few dry valleys in the mountains, Antarctica is covered by a huge sheet of snow and ice. In some places, the ice is nearly 2 miles (3.2 kilometers) thick.

Antarctica is the coldest, windiest place on Earth. Because the continent gets very little precipitation, it is also known as the world's largest cold desert.

A giant ice shelf

The Ross Ice Shelf is the largest ice shelf in Antarctica. It's about the size of France! In 2000, a huge chunk broke off and fell into the sea. It was 170 miles (272 km) long and 25 miles (40 km) wide!

The edge of the Ross Ice Shelf

The highest mountain

Vinson Massif is the highest mountain in Antarctica. Instead of having one tall peak, it has many. The tallest is 16,067 feet (4,900 meters). Because of its height and location, Vinson Massif is very cold. The average summer temperature is about minus 20 degrees Fahrenheit (minus 29 degrees Celsius).

One of Vinson Massif's snow-covered peaks

The Southern Ocean

The Southern Ocean is the second-smallest ocean in the world. It surrounds Antarctica and borders no other continents. Its surface area is 7.8 million square miles (20.3 million square kilometers). The Southern Ocean is believed to be Earth's youngest ocean, at about 30 million years old.

There are billions of tiny creatures called krill in the Southern Ocean.

Major Landforms

● place of interest ----- ice shelf boundary ☐ ice cap 🏔 mountain ▨ ice shelf

Antarctic Circle

Southern Ocean

Queen Maud Land

Enderby Land

Antarctic Peninsula

Weddell Sea

Ronne Ice Shelf

ANTARCTICA

Amery Ice Shelf

Bellinghausen Sea

Ellsworth Land

Vinson Massif

Transantarctic Mountains

American Highland

● South Pole

Amundsen Sea

Marie Byrd Land

Ross Ice Shelf

McMurdo Station

Ross Sea

Mount Erebus

Wilkes Land

- About 90 percent of the world's ice lies in Antarctica.
- In the center of the continent, the average monthly temperature is between minus 20 and minus 60 degrees Fahrenheit (minus 29 and minus 51 degrees Celsius).
- From the South Pole, all directions are north.
- Mount Erebus is a volcano that rises from the Ross Sea. Despite the cold climate, a large lake of melted rock (lava) boils inside the volcano.

107

The Arctic

The Arctic is a large area of water, ice, and frozen land that surrounds the North Pole. It is often defined as the region within the Arctic Circle.

During the Arctic's short summer, the ice sheet shrinks. But in winter, when the temperature drops, the ice sheet grows again.

Several countries lie partly in the Arctic. These include Canada, Finland, Norway, Sweden, Russia, and the United States. Most of the island of Greenland also lies in the Arctic.

Land of the Midnight Sun

The area north of the Arctic Circle is often called the Land of the Midnight Sun. The sun shines 24 hours a day there in late June and early July. In December and January, however, the sky is dark nearly all day, and temperatures drop very low.

A time-lapse photo of the midnight sun over northern Sweden in the summer

Ice caves

Inside the glaciers of Greenland are mazes of ice caves. During the summer, the glaciers' surface ice begins to melt. Water rushes down the slopes and runs into deep cracks. It carves tunnels and caves in the glaciers.

The tunnels inside Greenland's glaciers glow blue.

The Arctic Ocean

The world's northern-most ocean, the Arctic Ocean, is the smallest of Earth's five oceans. Its surface area is 5.4 million square miles (14 million square kilometers). That's about one and a half times the size of the United States. The Arctic Ocean touches the continents of North America, Europe, and Asia.

The cold waters of the Arctic Ocean

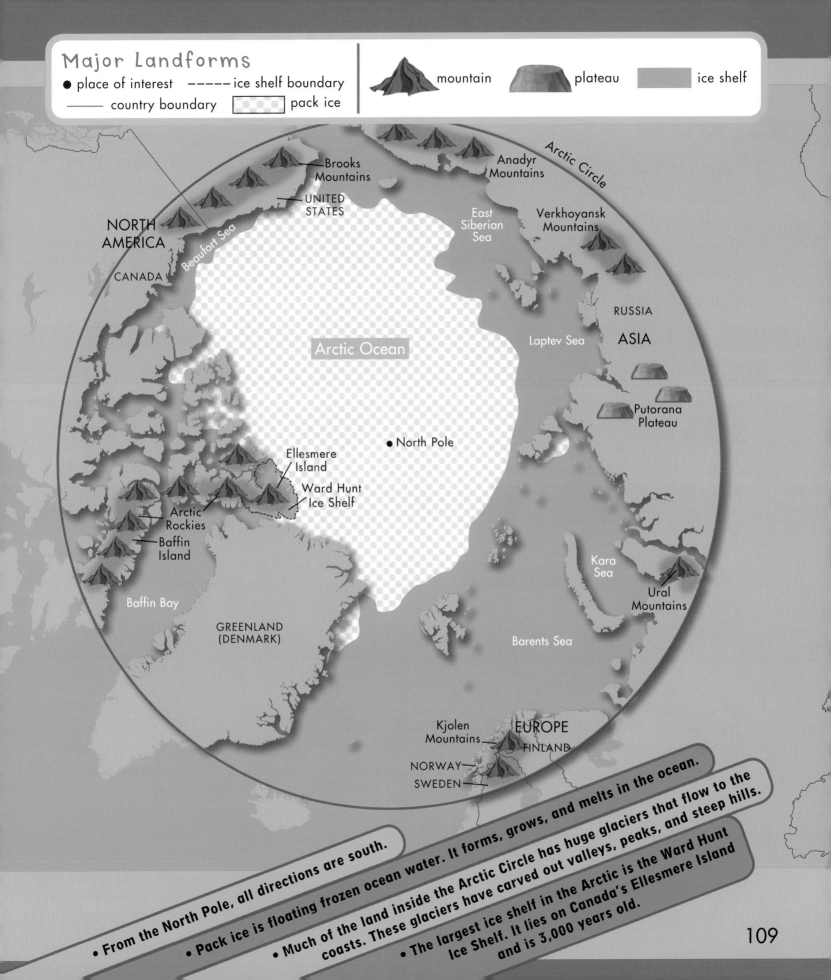

Major Landforms

- place of interest
- ----- ice shelf boundary
- —— country boundary
- pack ice
- mountain
- plateau
- ice shelf

Arctic Circle

Brooks Mountains

Anadyr Mountains

UNITED STATES

East Siberian Sea

Verkhoyansk Mountains

NORTH AMERICA

Beaufort Sea

CANADA

RUSSIA

Laptev Sea

ASIA

Arctic Ocean

Putorana Plateau

• North Pole

Ellesmere Island

Ward Hunt Ice Shelf

Arctic Rockies

Baffin Island

Kara Sea

Baffin Bay

Ural Mountains

GREENLAND (DENMARK)

Barents Sea

Kjolen Mountains

EUROPE

FINLAND

NORWAY

SWEDEN

- From the North Pole, all directions are south.
- Pack ice is floating frozen ocean water. It forms, grows, and melts in the ocean.
- Much of the land inside the Arctic Circle has huge glaciers that flow to the coasts. These glaciers have carved out valleys, peaks, and steep hills.
- The largest ice shelf in the Arctic is the Ward Hunt Ice Shelf. It lies on Canada's Ellesmere Island and is 3,000 years old.

Plants of Antarctica and the Arctic

Few plants can grow in Antarctica. Those that do are small and grow close to the coasts. Much of the continent's ground is hard and cold, making it difficult for plants to grow long roots.

The many hundreds of plants in the Arctic region are well-adapted to the forest and tundra ecosystems. An ecosystem is all of the living and nonliving things in a certain area. It includes plants, animals, soil, weather ... everything!

Some Plants of Antarctica

ice cap

lichen

Lichen is a mosslike plant that grows mostly on the rocky coasts of Antarctica. But it has been found on rocks close to the South Pole, too.

moss

Mosses are some of the oldest plants in Antarctica. They grow in wet, low-lying areas along the coasts.

Some Plants of the Arctic

forest

pine tree

Pine trees are a type of evergreen tree called a conifer. They have needlelike leaves and produce cones.

cranberry

Cranberry creeps over the floor of the northern forests. It has pink flowers and small red berries.

arctic poppy

Yellow and white poppies grow in Arctic forests and meadows. They turn their heads toward the sun.

tundra

cotton grass

Cotton grass grows in wet areas of the tundra. It has a white, feathery flower that breaks apart and blows away with the wind.

liverwort

Liverwort is a small, low-growing plant. It attaches itself to the ground or to rocks with thin threads instead of roots.

dwarf willow

The dwarf willow is the smallest tree in the world. It grows only 4 inches (10 centimeters) tall.

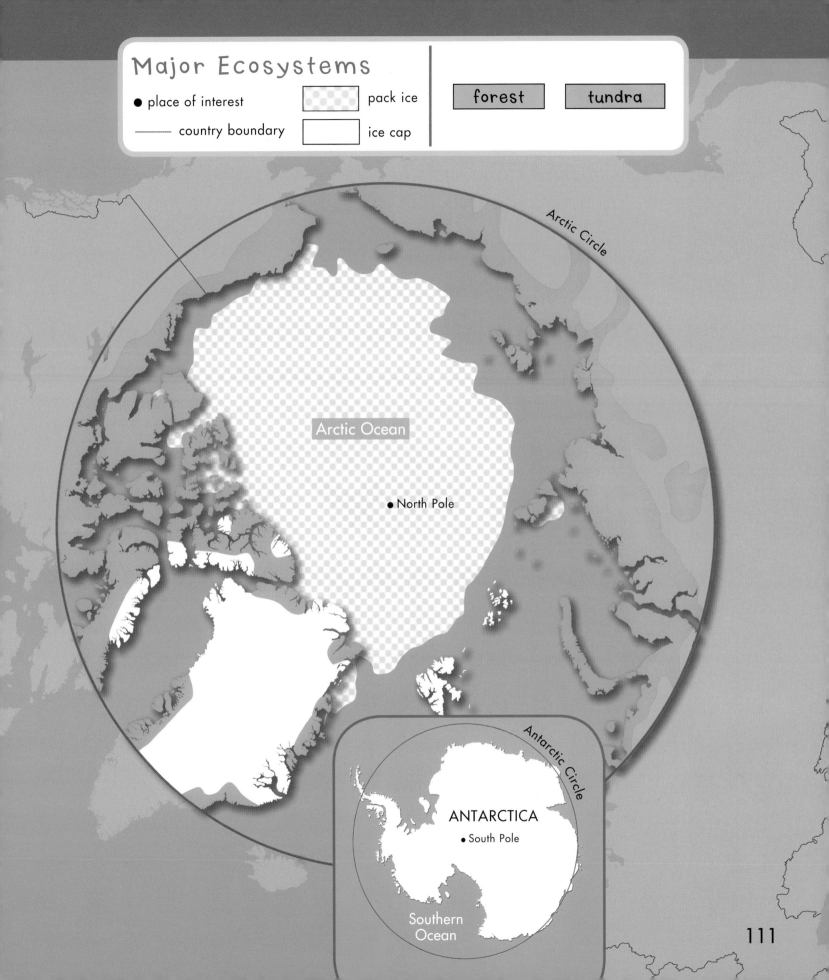

Major Ecosystems

● place of interest

—— country boundary

▨ pack ice

☐ ice cap

forest

tundra

Arctic Circle

Arctic Ocean

● North Pole

Antarctic Circle

ANTARCTICA

● South Pole

Southern Ocean

111

Animals of Antarctica and the Arctic

It is too cold for animals to live in central Antarctica. But around the continent's warmer coasts are plenty of penguins and other birds, fish, and seals.

Polar bears live on pack ice in the Arctic. But most other Arctic animals live in the region's tundra and forest ecosystems. An ecosystem is all of the living and nonliving things in a certain area.

Some Animals of Antarctica

ice cap

	emperor penguin	Male emperor penguins warm their mates' eggs on their feet throughout the bitterly cold Antarctic winter.
	icefish	Icefish live in Antarctic waters. Their bodies make a special liquid that stops their blood from freezing.
	petrel	The petrel is white with black eyes. It nests on icebergs off Antarctica's rocky shores.
	elephant seal	Elephant seals are huge and have large, floppy noses. Male elephant seals are fierce fighters.

Some Animals of the Arctic

forest

	ermine	The ermine's body is long and slender. It can easily chase mice and other prey through narrow underground tunnels.
	wolverine	The wolverine has big, furry feet that act like snowshoes. They keep the animal from sinking into the snow.
	brown bear	The brown bear lives in the forests of Russia. It feeds on roots, nuts, berries, fish, and small animals.

pack ice

	polar bear	Polar bears prowl the ice in the Arctic. They build snow caves to shelter their young.

tundra

	reindeer	Reindeer move across the Arctic in herds. Some herds may include thousands of reindeer.
	arctic hare	In the winter, the arctic hare's fur turns white. It sits so still on the snow that it is almost invisible to other animals.
	musk ox	The musk ox has a thick overcoat of long, shaggy hair that hangs down to the ground.

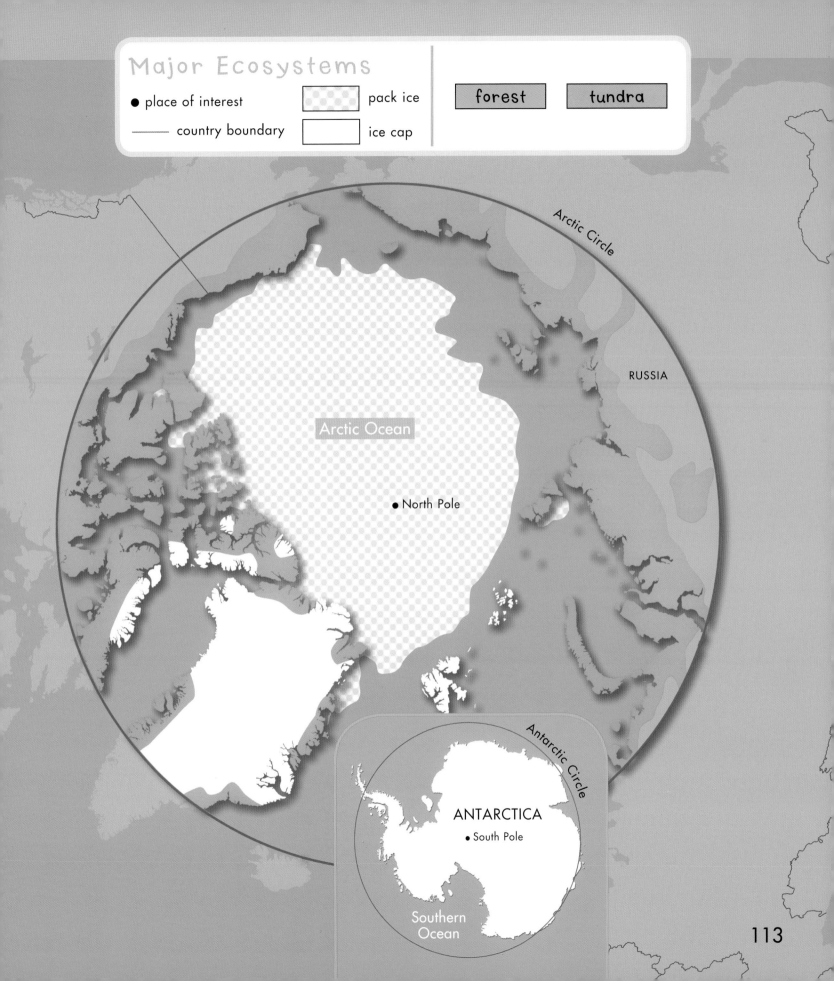

Major Ecosystems

- ● place of interest
- —— country boundary
- ▦ pack ice
- ☐ ice cap
- forest
- tundra

Arctic Circle

RUSSIA

Arctic Ocean

● North Pole

Antarctic Circle

ANTARCTICA

● South Pole

Southern
Ocean

The Five Oceans

About 97 percent of all water in the world is in Earth's five oceans: the Pacific Ocean, the Atlantic Ocean, the Indian Ocean, the Arctic Ocean, and the Southern Ocean. The largest of the oceans is the Pacific Ocean.

The average depth of the oceans is 12,460 feet (3,800 meters) or about 10 Empire State Buildings stacked on top of each other.

Each ocean has layers, or zones. Each zone has its own animals and plants. There are more than 1 million known species of ocean plants and animals.

Salty water

The oceans have always been salty. Long ago, rain poured onto Earth for millions of years. The rainwater formed rivers that flowed to low areas of land. The rainwater pooled there and formed oceans. When the rainwater ran over rocks, it took in salt, and that made the ocean water salty.

High and low tides

The moon and sun pull on Earth. The moon's pull causes the surface of an ocean to rise. Ocean water swells toward the moon when the moon is closest to it. This causes a high tide. The ocean water falls when the moon is farther away. This causes a low tide. During high tide, the pulling motion causes the water on the opposite side of the planet to also swell. The Earth spins around once in a day, so an ocean has two high tides in one day.

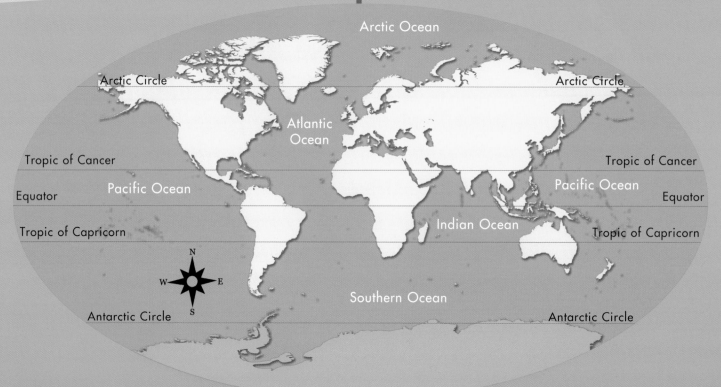

Some Plants and Animals of the Oceans

	dolphin	Dolphins are warm-blooded animals and use lungs to breathe. They are one of the few mammals that spend their entire lives in water.
	plankton	Plankton are tiny plants and animals that live near the surface of the ocean. They float through the water together in large masses.
	tuna	Tuna are one of the fastest fish in the world, reaching speeds of up to 45 miles (72 kilometers) per hour.
	blue whale	With a length of up to 100 feet (31 m) and a weight of more than 150 tons (135 metric tons), the blue whale is believed to be the largest animal on Earth.
	jellyfish	Jellyfish have no bones and look like floating bags of water. Some of them glow.
	viper fish	The viper fish lives deep in the ocean during the day. But at night, it moves to shallower water to eat. It has a giant mouth and long, sharp teeth.
	gulper eel	The gulper eel has a long, thin body that helps it hide easily from other animals. Its dark coloring also helps it hide in the dark midnight zone.
	kelp	Kelp is a type of seaweed that grows in cold ocean water. It is brown or green and can grow to be 100 feet (31 m) long.

sunlit zone

twilight zone

midnight zone

ocean floor

The Ocean Floor

The land under Earth's oceans is not flat and sandy. In fact, it's very much like the dry land of the continents. It's made up of tall mountains, deep valleys, and wide, flat plains.

The ocean floor is an amazing place. The tallest landform and lowest point on Earth are found in the ocean.

The world's tallest mountain is Mount Kea in Hawaii. From the base at the bottom of the Pacific Ocean to its peak high in the sky, this mountain measures 33,476 feet (10,210 meters). While Mount Everest and other peaks are higher above sea level, Mount Kea is the tallest from bottom to top.

The world's lowest point is the Mariana Trench, which lies in the Pacific Ocean. At 35,840 feet (10,931 m) deep, it is deeper than Mount Everest—the highest mountain on land—is tall.

Continental shelf

A continental shelf is the flat, underwater edge of a continent. These shelves can be from 50 miles (80 kilometers) wide to 900 miles (1,440 km) wide. Continental shelves make up about 50 percent of the Arctic Ocean floor. No other ocean floor has as many continental shelves.

Continental slope

The outer part of the continental shelf begins to slope before it makes a steep drop to the ocean floor. The steep drop is called the continental slope, which is the true edge of a continent.

Abyssal plain

The smooth, nearly flat area of the ocean floor is called the abyssal plain. It starts at the bottom of the continental slope. This is truly the bottom of the ocean.

Underwater volcanoes

The oceans even have volcanoes! The Mariana Arc is a chain of underwater volcanoes in the Pacific Ocean. A volcano is a type of mountain that can throw hot, melted rock (lava), ashes, and gases from deep inside Earth. Volcanoes can erupt at ocean ridges and trenches. When they erupt above sea level, they form volcanic islands.

- Most islands began as volcanoes. The Hawaiian Islands formed when volcanoes erupted under the Pacific Ocean.
- More than half of the volcanoes in the world are found underwater and on land around the rim of the Pacific Ocean. This circle is called the Ring of Fire.
- There are mountains in every ocean. If placed together, they would form a chain more than 37,300 miles (59,680 km) long.

Mid-ocean ridge

The mid-ocean ridge is a mountain chain with the most active volcanic area on Earth. Deep in the ocean, it winds its way around the continents. It's four times as long as the continents' major mountain ranges (the Andes, the Rocky Mountains, and the Himalayas) combined.

Sea trench

Sea trenches are large valleys in the ocean floor. They are formed when two moving sections of Earth's floor meet, and one slides beneath the other. Because of this movement, deep-sea trenches are the most active part of the deep ocean.

Seamount

A seamount is an underwater mountain with a height of at least 3,300 feet (1,000 m). Most seamounts are volcanoes with peaks that do not reach the surface of the ocean. More than 50 percent of all seamounts are in the Pacific Ocean.

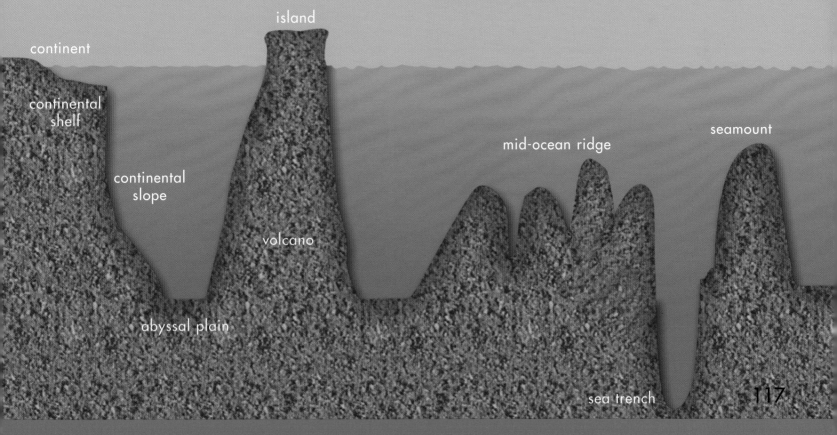

island

continent

continental shelf

continental slope

mid-ocean ridge

seamount

volcano

abyssal plain

sea trench

Ocean Climate

Oceans affect the world's weather and climate. Warm currents, or streams of ocean water, bring a mild climate to the nearby land. Cold currents bring a cool climate.

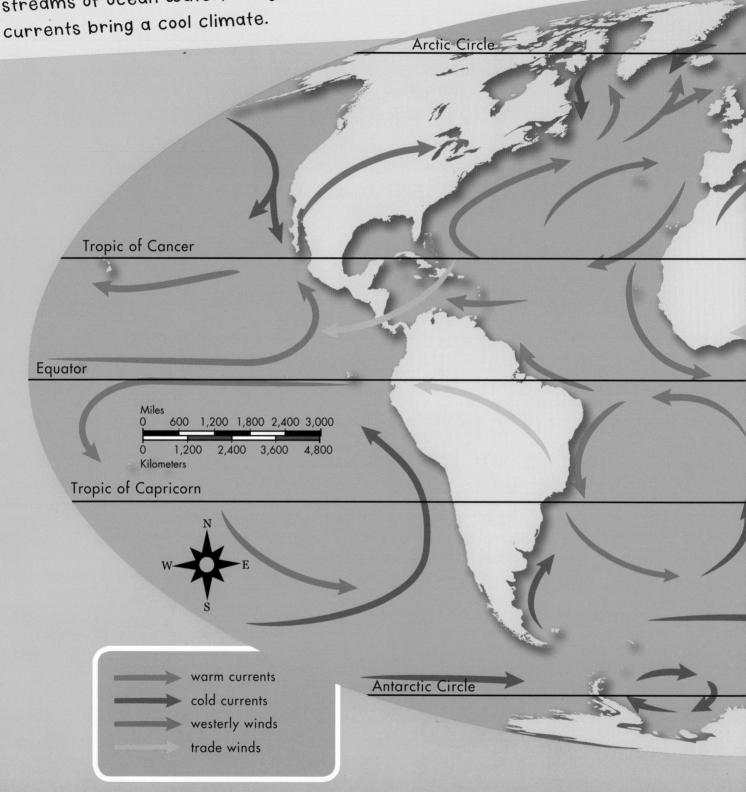

Arctic Circle

Tropic of Cancer

Equator

Miles
0   600   1,200   1,800   2,400   3,000

0   1,200   2,400   3,600   4,800
Kilometers

Tropic of Capricorn

N
W   E
S

Antarctic Circle

warm currents
cold currents
westerly winds
trade winds

Winds also affect the world's weather and climate. They blow from various directions, bringing anything from cool breezes to hot and steamy air masses. Westerly winds blow from the west to the east. Trade winds blow almost constantly in one direction, usually toward the equator from the east.

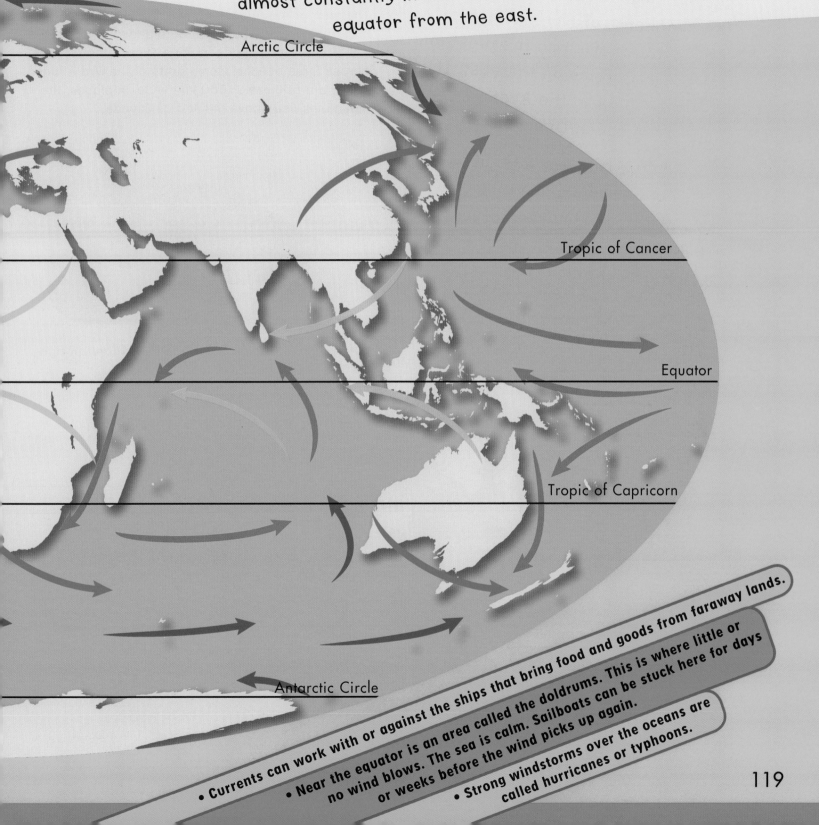

Arctic Circle

Tropic of Cancer

Equator

Tropic of Capricorn

Antarctic Circle

• Currents can work with or against the ships that bring food and goods from faraway lands.

• Near the equator is an area called the doldrums. This is where little or no wind blows. The sea is calm. Sailboats can be stuck here for days or weeks before the wind picks up again.

• Strong windstorms over the oceans are called hurricanes or typhoons.

Atlantic Ocean

The Atlantic Ocean is the world's second-largest ocean. It borders the continents of North America and South America on the west and Europe and Africa on the east. It also touches both the Arctic Ocean and the Southern Ocean.

The Atlantic Ocean's total area is about 34 million square miles (88.4 million square kilometers). Its deepest point lies 28,232 feet (8,611 meters) below the surface.

Mid-Atlantic Ridge

The floor of the Atlantic Ocean is divided by the Mid-Atlantic Ridge, a chain of underwater mountains. It is part of the mid-ocean ridge system that snakes across three oceans. Some parts of the Mid-Atlantic Ridge are 500 miles (800 km) wide. In places, the mountains rise above the sea as islands.

An underwater volcano in the Mid-Atlantic Ridge erupted and formed an island.

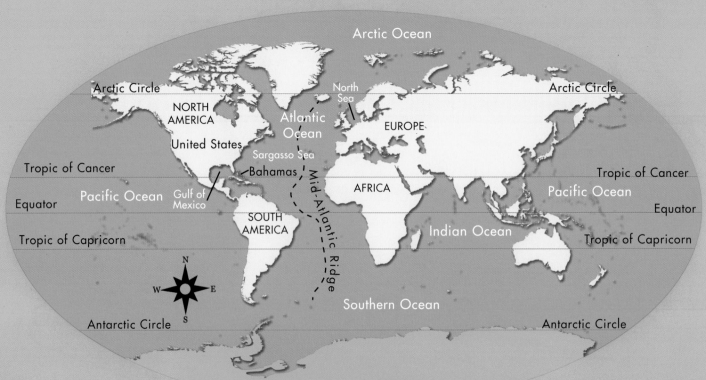

Sea grass meadows

Sea grass grows in the shallow, sunlit waters southeast of the United States. These underwater grass meadows are home to small animals. Baby seahorses hold on to blades of grass, and lobsters feed there before moving into deeper water.

Blue holes

The Bahamas is a chain of islands in the Atlantic Ocean that are southeast of the United States. The islands lie on soft rock banks. Long ago, these banks rose above sea level. Rainwater wore away the rock, making caves and canyons. Today, the holes are flooded with seawater and are called blue holes. Strange cave creatures called troglobites live here. Because the pools are so dark, the animals' skin is very pale. Many troglobites are blind or have no eyes at all.

There are more than 50 blue holes in the shallow water off the Bahamas.

Reef walls

The coast of Grand Bahama Island in the Bahamas is circled by a coral reef. The steep walls of the reef have caves. Sponges and sea fans, types of ocean animals, stick out from the walls.

Reef walls near the Bahamas

Seaweed jungles

In the clear, warm, and salty Sargasso Sea, in the middle of the North Atlantic, there are floating seaweed jungles. The seaweed has been pushed there by ocean currents. The Sargasso Sea is a breeding ground for eels and a home for loggerhead sea turtles that hatch off the North American coast.

Seaweed jungle, Sargasso Sea

- In the North Sea and Gulf of Mexico, huge amounts of oil and natural gas are trapped under the rocks of the ocean floor. The oil and gas were formed from the mineral remains of dead sea creatures.
- The Atlantic Ocean makes up 17 percent of Earth's total surface area.

Pacific Ocean

The Pacific Ocean is the largest of the five oceans. In fact, it covers almost one-third of Earth's surface.

The Pacific Ocean's borders touch many countries. Its southern border touches the Southern Ocean. Its northern border is the Bering Sea.

The deepest place on Earth is found in the Pacific Ocean. It reaches 35,840 feet (10,931 meters) below the surface of the water.

Strong storms and volcanic eruptions take place in Pacific Ocean waters.

Worm city

Giant red worms live inside white tubes attached to huge hot-water vents on the ocean floor. The worms feed on the minerals inside the vents. The vents also support many animals such as clams, mussels, and shrimps.

Giant tube worms live in vents on the ocean floor.

Black smokers

At the bottom of the Pacific Ocean, hot water full of minerals pours from towering tunnels. The water is warmed by hot rocks inside vents, or cracks, in the ocean floor. The minerals harden around the vents as the hot water cools. As more minerals are laid down, the tunnels grow taller and taller. They are called black smokers because dark-colored minerals from the vents turn the water black.

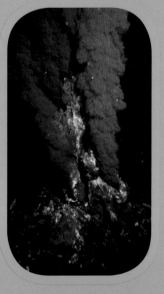

A black smoker

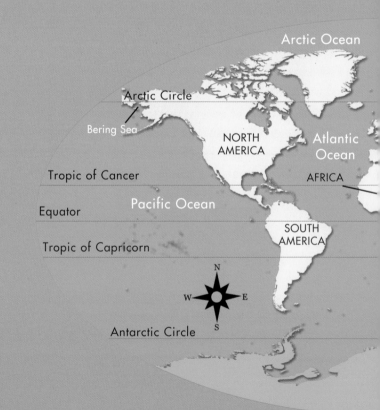

Arctic Ocean

Arctic Circle

Bering Sea

NORTH AMERICA

Atlantic Ocean

Tropic of Cancer

AFRICA

Equator

Pacific Ocean

SOUTH AMERICA

Tropic of Capricorn

N W E S

Antarctic Circle

Indian Ocean

The third-largest ocean in the world is the Indian Ocean. It touches Australia on the east and Africa on the west. Asia is to the north, and the Southern Ocean is to the south.

The total surface area of the Indian Ocean is 26.6 million square miles (69.2 million square kilometers).

Important sea routes in the Indian Ocean connect Africa and Asia with Europe, North America, and South America.

The Sunda Arc

The islands of Sumatra and Java in the Indian Ocean form the spine of the Sunda Arc. The Sundra Arc is a chain of volcanoes that are regularly shaken by earthquakes and tidal waves. A volcano is a kind of mountain that can throw hot, melted rock (lava), ashes, and gases from deep inside Earth.

Smoke rises from Mount Bromo, Java.

Bay of Bengal

In the northeastern Indian Ocean is the Bay of Bengal. Tropical storms move from the ocean to land. Sometimes the storms cause the rivers in the area to flood.

Flooding of the Ganges River near the Bay of Bengal

123

Protecting the Environment

Experts agree that global warming is quickly changing the planet. The seas are getting warmer. Near the poles, this warmer water causes the ice caps to gradually melt. It also causes glaciers to flow into the oceans much faster than before. Rising sea water and melting ice take away the homes and food sources of many animals.

Scientists say global warming is caused by pollution from humans. Pollution is made up of harmful materials and wastes. Fishing, hunting, oil spills, and other human activities also harm oceans and polar areas. But many people are working to protect the poles and oceans.

Stories in the ice

Scientists dig down into the ice to find traces of the past. Each layer of ice represents a single year of snowfall, including everything that fell into the snow—dust, ash, gases, and more. Ice cores taken from under the surface of Greenland's ice show that the air has been polluted with lead from gasoline for many years.

Scientists collect ice cores by driving a hollow tube deep into the thick ice sheets of Antarctica, Greenland, and other polar areas.

A polar bear jumps from one chunk of ice to another.

Bears on ice

Global warming is a threat to polar bears. The bears depend on an icy platform to hunt for seals. But as the ice melts, they have to swim farther and farther away to catch their prey. Warmer weather shortens the bears' hunting season, which can cause bears to starve.

Antarctica: the last wilderness

In 1959, more than 40 countries agreed to the Antarctic Treaty. This protects the continent because it only allows peaceful and scientific use. The land of Antarctica is protected from mining and oil drilling. The animals there are also protected. Still, wildlife is hurt by illegal fishing and poaching, which is illegal hunting or stealing of animals. Also, some people want to use Antarctica's rich resources. But scientists say mining and oil drilling could greatly damage the continent's plant and animal life.

Oil slicks harm ocean life

Every day, tankers criss-cross the oceans carrying huge amounts of oil. Sometimes there are accidents, and oil spills into the water. The oil spreads across the surface in huge slicks. These slicks can kill ocean life and destroy coastlines. Animals such as seabirds are coated with thick oil so they can't fly or breathe properly.

Every year, millions of gallons of oil spill into the world's oceans. Cleanup is a difficult task.

Saving the whales

People around the world are working to protect whales. Like humans, whales are mammals. They breathe air and feed milk to their young. For many years, whales were hunted freely. Great numbers were killed. Laws were finally made to protect whales. The number of whales is slowly growing, but they face threats other than hunting. Collisions with ships and the effects of pollution harm whales. But getting tangled in fishing gear is the biggest danger to whales.

A humpback whale

Risks of overfishing

Every year millions of tons of fish are caught for food. While humans need food, taking too many fish will mean trouble in the future. As schools of fish are detected with high-tech equipment, large drift nets are cast out. These nets stretch far and deep through the sea waters. They catch almost anything in their path. Overfishing means young fish are taken before they have had a chance to reproduce. Also, seals, dolphins, whales, and turtles get tangled in the nets. These animals often die before they can be freed.

Index